WHODUNNIT

Forensics

C.M. Johnson

full tilt
PRESS

Forensics
Origins: Whodunnit

Full Tilt Press
42982 Osgood Road
Fremont, CA 94539
www.readfulltilt.com

Full Tilt Press publications may be purchased for educational, business, or sales promotional use.

Editorial Credits
Design and layout by Sara Radka
Edited by Lauren Dupuis-Perez
Copyedited by Renae Gilles

Image Credits
Getty Images: iStockphoto, 4, 7, 13, 14, 17, 24, 34, 41, 43; Newscom: CSU Archives/Everett Collection, 10, CSU Archives/Everett Collection, 11, Ed Hille/Philadelphia Inquirer/MCT, 26, Hartswood Films/BBC Wales / Album, 31, Jean-Claude Ernst/ UPI Photo Service, 33, Red Huber/Orlando Sentinel/MCT, 37, Splash News, 36, UPI Photo/Monika Graff, 12, ZUMAPRESS/Keystone Pictures USA, 6, ZUMAPRESS/Randy Pench/Sacramento Bee, 29; Shutterstock: Africa Studio, 5, Andrey_Popov, 39, bikeriderlondon, 23, bikeriderlondon, 27, Comaniciu Dan, 44, Couperfield, 40, Dimarion, 28, Edw, 38, Hein Nouwens, 8, Henrik Dolle, 25, kilukilu, 20, kilukilu, 21, Luis Louro, 35, Peshkova, 19, Pinkyone, 9, Pyty, 16, Saivann, 30, Vecteezy: background and cover elements; Wikimedia: Fr. Šjv., 18

ISBN: 978-1-62920-612-7 (library binding)
ISBN: 978-1-62920-624-0 (eBook)

Printed in the United States of America.

Contents

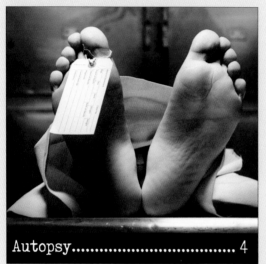

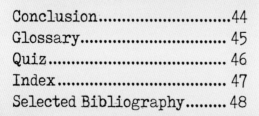

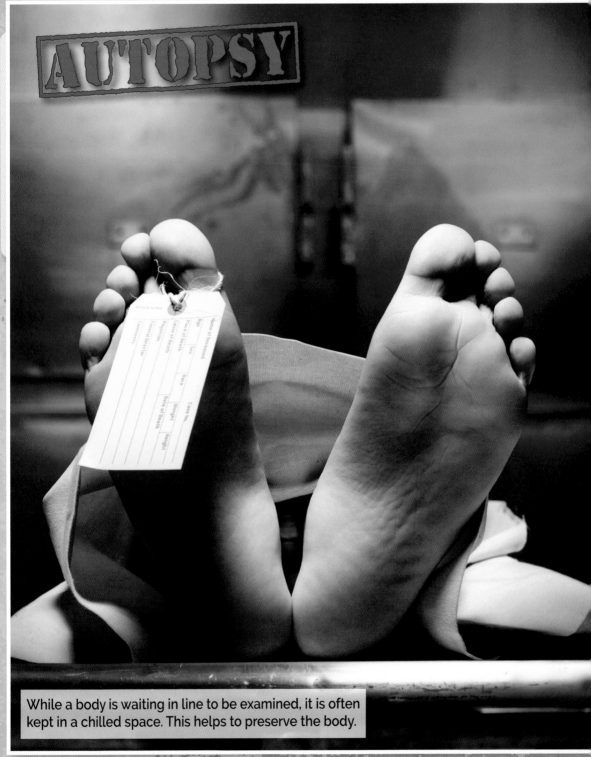

AUTOPSY

While a body is waiting in line to be examined, it is often kept in a chilled space. This helps to preserve the body.

Introduction

A gem is stolen. A dead body is found. In Europe in the 1200s, crimes like these were not investigated the way they are now. Instead, the victim's family fought the family accused of the crime. Later, a practice called a "trial by ordeal" was used. Suspects put their hands into boiling water. A few days later, judges then looked at the wounds. God was said to heal the innocent. Infection meant guilt.

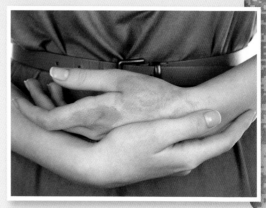

In a "trial by ordeal," the worse a crime was, the deeper a suspect was forced to plunge their hand into a large cooking pot of boiling water.

In other parts of the world at this time, people were using clues to solve crimes. In 1247 in China, a man named Sung Tz'u wrote a book on **forensics**. Sung Tz'u lists ways to spot **foul play**. He discusses the way a body changes after death. He describes some of the first autopsies. In an autopsy, a body is studied both inside and out. Today, photos are taken at each step of the exam. A written report lists details that identify the body and tries to explain the cause of death.

DID YOU KNOW?

About 4,000 years ago, one of the first laws that asked for evidence as proof of a crime was written by King Hammurabi of Babylon.

forensics: the results of a scientific test done to help solve a crime

foul play: criminal violence, murder, or dishonest acts

François-Eugène Vidocq's life and his work as a detective have inspired books, TV shows, and movies in both English and French.

Forensics in Action

In 1812, Paris police put François-Eugène Vidocq at the head of one of the world's first detective agencies. Vidocq had once been a crook. He had **forged** documents. He had started fights. He knew all the great criminals of France, and he could think like a thief. This made him a very good spy. In 1822, a woman named Isabelle d'Arcy was shot to death. Police said d'Arcy's rich husband had done it. D'Arcy was seeing another man. Maybe her husband had gone into a jealous rage.

forge: to illegally create or change a document

Vidocq had other ideas. D'Arcy's jewelry was gone. Would her husband have stolen jewels he had bought himself? Vidocq suspected the boyfriend, and he ordered an autopsy to prove it. He and the undertaker had to do it secretly. At that time in France, cutting into a body was **taboo**. People did not want to **defile** the dead. But Vidocq showed how an autopsy could let the dead find justice. The bullet taken from d'Arcy's skull did not match her husband's gun. It did match her boyfriend's. Faced with the findings, the guilty boyfriend confessed.

taboo: something that a culture or society bans or avoids

defile: to dishonor or to make something impure

Isabelle d'Arcy was found shot in her own apartment, a fact that made police suspect that she knew her killer.

History of Forensics

Even after death, people's bodies can still tell us a lot.

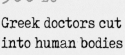

300 BC

Greek doctors cut into human bodies to study disease.

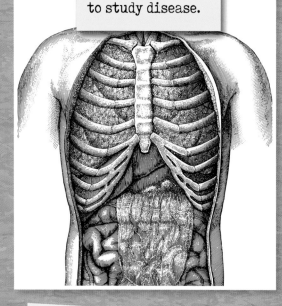

1231

In Rome, Emperor Frederick II passes a law that says human dissection is legal.

1247

In China, Sung Tz'u's handbook tells how to spot poisonings and strangulations by inspecting the body. The book is called *Hsi Yuan Chi Lu*. This means "The Washing Away of Wrongs."

1302

An official in Bologna, Italy, asks for an autopsy in a case of suspected poisoning.

1855

In Germany, Rudolph Virchow calls for the use of microscopes to study a body's cells. The practice is adopted in the study of both disease and crime.

1840

In France, tests are done on the stomach contents of the husband of Marie Lafarge. She is found guilty of poisoning him with arsenic, a chemical used to kill insects and weeds.

1918

As the first scientifically-trained chief medical examiner for New York City, Dr. Charles Norris works to create a criminal justice system that uses autopsy results and other forensic science.

1973

Martial artist and movie star Bruce Lee is found dead in China at the age of 32. Some suspect murder. But an autopsy shows he had a bad reaction to a prescription painkiller.

2015

As a result of the February 2015 case of Mushkooub Aubid, Minnesota governor Mark Dayton signs a state law that protects a family's right to protest an autopsy for religious reasons.

Crime and Autopsy

The death of a celebrity is big news. People want to know where stars were and who they were with when they died. Most of all, they want to know what happened. Fans eagerly await the autopsy report. But sometimes the report creates more mysteries. Such was the case with the gangster John Dillinger. In the early 1930s, Dillinger robbed a string of banks, killed a police officer, and broke out of jail. He was the FBI's "Public Enemy Number 1." In 1934, agents set up a trap, and a thief was shot down in Chicago. Soon after, many people saw the body. They followed it to the **morgue**. There, Dillinger's sister identified the body as her brother's. But today, some people say Dillinger was not really killed that day. They believe it was another man.

Reporters made Dillinger famous by writing about his clever robberies and fast escapes.

DID YOU KNOW?

As a child in Indianapolis, Indiana, John Dillinger played pranks with a group of boys who called themselves "The Dirty Dozen."

morgue: a place where bodies are kept before being identified or buried

That legend stems from the autopsy report. The writer Jay Robert Nash said there were differences between the report and what is known about Dillinger. The **coroner** said the body's eyes were brown. But many who knew Dillinger said his eyes were blue or gray.

Nash said a scar on Dillinger's face was not noted, nor was his missing tooth. Did the FBI lie about the man they shot? Nash still says yes, and he is not the only one.

coroner: an official whose job is to find the cause of death when people die in sudden, violent, or suspicious ways

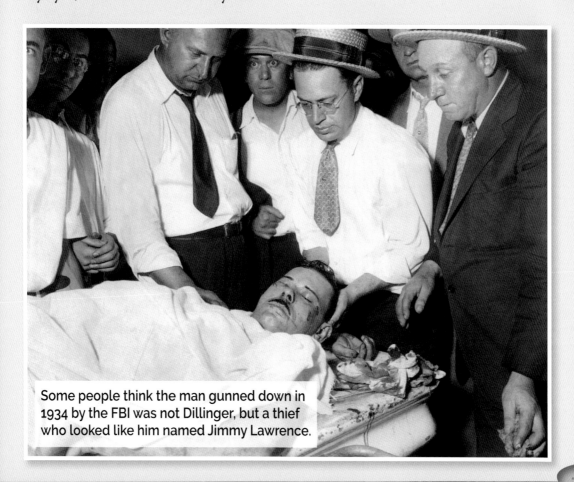

Some people think the man gunned down in 1934 by the FBI was not Dillinger, but a thief who looked like him named Jimmy Lawrence.

Studying human remains from the past can give us clues about a society's diet and its ability to treat illness.

Autopsy Today

We used to look at a body with only the naked eye. Now, we have microscopes. We can look at cells, and learn more about disease. We can see tiny traces on the skin. Each speck might be a clue. A yeast spore might tie a murder to a bakery. A hair might be from the pet of a thief. Examiners also use X-rays. These tools are even used to look at life and death in the past.

Recently, a "virtual autopsy" was done on the Egyptian King Tutankhamun, commonly known as King Tut. His body had been **mummified**. To look at it, scientists used CT scans. These are made up of X-rays taken from many angles. A computer puts the images together to get more details.

mummify: to preserve a body and wrap it in cloth

King Tut was born in 1341 BC. He took the throne as a child, and died at the age of 19. Before his CT scan, it was thought he had died in a chariot accident. A chariot is a two-wheeled cart that is drawn by a horse. The driver stands while guiding the cart. But Tut's scans show that it would have been impossible for him to drive a chariot. The king had a bone disease. He also had a **club foot**. He could stand only with a cane. Scientists now think he died of malaria, a fever found in the tropics.

club foot: a foot that is misshapen and twisted out of its natural position

MYSTERY SKELETON

In 2001, a skeleton was dug up on a Maryland farm. It was found under some trash. The bones were studied by forensic anthropologists. These are scientists who look at bones. The scientists use the information to identify the person. They look for clues to see if a crime was committed. The Maryland skeleton was that of a boy from the seventeenth century. Experts think he was a servant. They think he was beaten by the family he worked for, and when he died of his injuries, they hid his body.

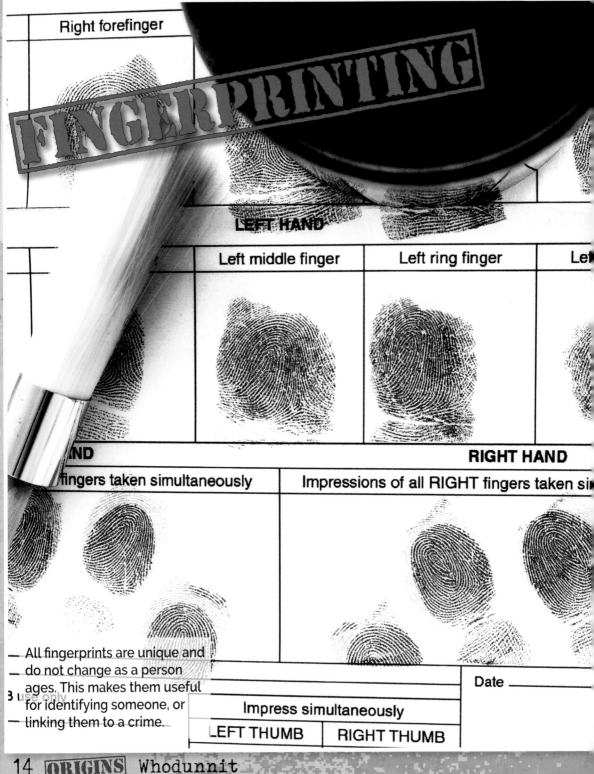

Right forefinger

FINGERPRINTING

LEFT HAND

Left middle finger	Left ring finger	Le...

...ND

RIGHT HAND

...fingers taken simultaneously

Impressions of all RIGHT fingers taken si...

All fingerprints are unique and do not change as a person ages. This makes them useful for identifying someone, or linking them to a crime.

...use only

Date _____

Impress simultaneously

LEFT THUMB	RIGHT THUMB

Introduction

Look closely at your finger. You will see tiny grooves. These lines cover our hands and feet. They help us grip things. Our fingers are also covered with sweat glands. Sweat clings to these lines like ink, causing us to leave traces of ourselves wherever we go. Since no two fingerprints are the same, those traces are like signatures. China was ahead of most of the rest of the world when it came to this discovery. As early as AD 700, people in China used fingerprints as signatures. Europe and South America caught up in the mid-1800s.

People in ancient Babylon, a city in the area of modern-day Iraq, "signed" contracts with their fingerprints about 4,000 years ago.

When studying crimes, police use the "theory of **transfer**." When two objects meet, some trace of that meeting can be found. That trace might be a fingerprint. Once it is found, this trace can be "read." It might tell us when something happened. It can clue us into a chain of events. Most of all, police hope it can tell them who was there at the scene of the crime.

transfer: to pass from one person, place, or thing to another

In the late 1800s, a famous **serial killer** named "Jack the Ripper" killed at least five women in the Whitechapel area of London.

Forensics in Action

In the early 1900s, the people of London were afraid. Several recent murders had gone unsolved. The London police had even failed to catch the terrible Jack the Ripper. In 1902, when two shopkeepers were beaten to death, police felt the pressure to find this killer. The public's faith in them was at stake. But the police had nothing to go on to solve this new crime. Then an officer saw an oval smudge on a cash box. He gave it to Charles Collins.

DID YOU KNOW?

In notes that were printed in London newspapers, "Jack the Ripper" made fun of the police for failing to catch him.

serial killer: someone who murders three or more people over a period of time, with breaks between the killings

Collins was in **Scotland Yard**'s fingerprint division. The division was only one year old. Collins was eager to try out his new system. He felt let down when the fingerprint did not match any others he had on file. But when brothers Alfred and Albert Stratton became suspects, Collins found a match. The cash box print had been made by Alfred's thumb. In 1905, the case went to trial. The police were nervous. The public did not know very much about fingerprints. Just a few months before, prints had been used for the first time to convict a person in an English court. But he was a **petty** thief. Would a jury find two men guilty of murder based on a smudge? Would they go free? Would the Yard get blasted for messing up another case? On May 23, 1905, the jury gave a thumbs-up to the new technology. The men were found guilty and hanged.

Scotland Yard: the headquarters of the London police force

petty: small or not very important

To make a print visible on a hard surface like a metal cash box, police use a soft brush to dust powder over the area.

History of Forensics

Even after fingerprints were discovered, hundreds of years passed before it was well-known that they could be used in fighting crime.

1684

In England, Dr. Nehemiah Grew writes about his work using one of the first microscopes to spot the ridge patterns on fingertips.

AD 700

In China, fingerprints are used to identify documents and clay sculptures.

1823

In Poland, professor Jan Evangelista Purkyně notes that fingerprint patterns fall into several types.

1880

In a letter to the journal Nature, Scottish missionary Henry Faulds urges Scotland Yard to use fingerprints to tag criminals.

1892

In Argentina, police use fingerprints to get a confession out of a mother who killed her two children. News of the case does not reach Europe for many years.

1897

In India, Azizul Haque invents an effective way to classify fingerprints. This makes them a good tool for the police.

1904

The United States Bureau of Identification creates a fingerprint database.

1911

Thomas Jennings is the first American convicted of murder in the United States based on fingerprint evidence.

1980–1985

The Japanese National Police Agency creates the world's first computerized fingerprint database.

2011

The FBI replaces its fingerprint computer with Advanced Fingerprint Identification Technology (AFIT). The new system improves matching accuracy from 92% to 99.6%.

Fingerprint cards bear the marks of every finger. Each print on a person's hand might vary due to a scar or an injury.

Crime and Fingerprinting

Even after it was discovered that fingerprints are unique marks, it would take a long time before they could be used as a standard tool for solving crimes. Fingerprints fall into three main types. These are arches, loops, and **whorls**. Before this find, police had to look at each print on file to spot a match. Eventually, police began to file the prints by type. This made the task quicker.

whorl: a pattern in the shape of a circle or a swirl around a central point

SIMPSON CASE

In court, evidence is only as strong as the care police take with it. In 1994, Nicole Simpson and Ron Goldman were found stabbed to death near Los Angeles. Simpson's husband O.J., a former football star, was charged. Evidence pointed to O.J. But police made some mistakes. They used a phone in the house. This might have destroyed fingerprints. They put a blanket over Nicole Simpson's body. This **compromised** fiber evidence. O.J. was found not guilty.

Police look for other marks as well. Shoe prints and tire tracks can also help catch a crook. A tire mark can help identify a car. A trail of shoe prints can reveal a limp. If police have a suspect, they can match a **tread** at the scene to that person's shoe or car. At a crime scene, photos are taken of all the tracks. Sometimes, casts are made. A cast can show more detail than a photo. To make a cast, the print is filled with plaster. Prints in snow are sprayed with wax, then filled with plaster that has been chilled. Prints on flat, dry surfaces are not as easy to find. But once one is spotted, a copy can be "lifted" from a wood floor or the hard ground. One method is to use sticky gel on a piece of cloth.

compromise: to reduce in value or usefulness

tread: the impressed pattern left from the shoe of a person walking or a tire rolling over the ground

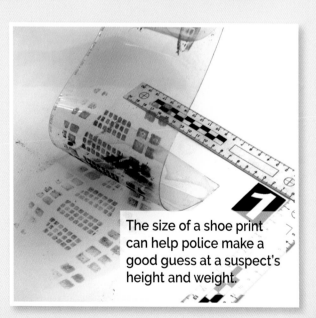

The size of a shoe print can help police make a good guess at a suspect's height and weight.

Fingerprinting Today

Technology has come a long way since 1902 and Charles Collins's paper file of fingerprints. Prints are still taken with ink in some police departments, but others use "live scan" devices. Scans have more detail. The images are printed on a card or loaded directly into a database. The FBI's Next Generation Identification (NGI) system stores fingerprints, palm prints, and images of eyes and faces.

Today, fingerprints can also be used to solve decades-old cases. In 2014, the police in Salt Lake City, Utah, looked at a **cold case**. A woman had been murdered in 1991. The killer had done an odd thing. He had left LEGO™ blocks on the floor of the home. At the time, police could not identify a print on one of the blocks. In 2014, they tested it again. This time, they got a match. In 1991, the person's prints were not in the system yet. That was because he was only five years old at the time. His father had brought him to the crime scene. The killer may have used his son as a **ruse** to get into the house. The son's print led police to his father, who was already in jail for another crime.

cold case: a crime that has been left unsolved for a long time

ruse: a trick or lie used to get someone to do something

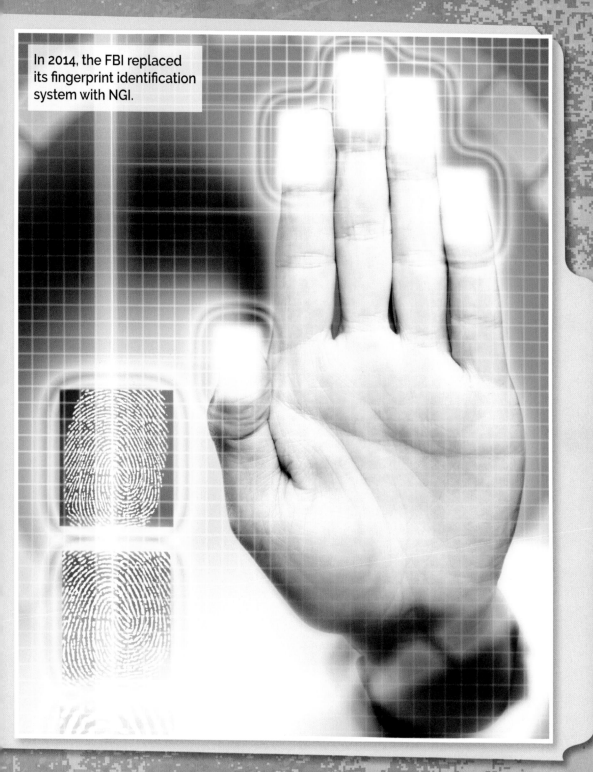

In 2014, the FBI replaced its fingerprint identification system with NGI.

In the early 1900s, scientists found that an unknown blood sample could be identified by the way it affected or reacted to other substances.

Introduction

A **grisly** discovery is made. There is a big pool of blood in the snow. Has a person been killed? Should police start looking for a body? Maybe. Maybe not. Perhaps a wolf killed a deer. Maybe a farmer butchered a hog. Before blood testing, police had no way to know if blood was from a human or an animal. They also could not tell blood from other substances. Could it be paint or dye? In the 1900s, scientists began to create blood tests that answered these questions. In 1901, the discovery of blood types helped police rule out possible victims. In the 1960s–80s, blood testing took another step forward. Scientists now had very strong microscopes. They could look at tiny parts of the blood. They found that certain proteins were unique to an individual. Blood had a "fingerprint" called DNA.

DNA tests are performed using physical samples such as a person's blood, spit, or bone.

DID YOU KNOW?

DNA, short for deoxyribonucleic acid, provides the code that determines traits such as eye and skin color.

grisly: something that inspires disgust and fear

People who are arrested are photographed so that their pictures can be kept on file and used in future investigations.

Forensics in Action

On July 9, 1977, police near Chicago, Illinois, saw a girl on the side of the road. Cathleen Crowell was 16. Her clothes were torn and her skin was scratched. She said she had been dragged into a car and attacked. At the police station, Crowell pointed to a photo in a **mug book**, and a man named Gary Dotson was arrested. At the trial, he was found guilty and sent to jail.

mug book: a police file of "mug shots," or photos taken of people who have been arrested

Then, in 1985, Crowell spoke up. She was feeling guilty. She had made up the whole story. She had gotten all the details of the attack from a book. But **prosecutors** did not believe her. Finally, in 1987, Dotson's lawyer read an article about a new blood test. DNA evidence had been used to find a killer in Great Britain. Could it also be used to free an innocent man? A test in the spring of 1988 was not a success. The DNA samples from 1977 had **degraded**. They did not give a good result. Luckily, a new DNA test was being used in California. It worked on old samples. The new test showed Dotson was not guilty. In 1989, he was cleared of all charges.

prosecutor: the lawyer who is responsible for making a case against a person who has been charged with a crime

degrade: when something's properties or parts break down or wear away

The Cetus Corporation in California patented the PCR test, which could be used to identify old DNA samples, in the mid-1980s.

History of Forensics

Scientists did not understand DNA or the information found in blood until very recently.

1900

In Germany, Paul Uhlenhuth creates the precipitin test, which can tell if blood is from a human or an animal. It can also tell blood from other substances.

1901

In Austria, Karl Landsteiner discovers that human blood can be grouped into four main types.

1904

In Germany, Uhlenhuth's blood-testing technique leads to the conviction of Ludwig Tessnow for the murders of four children.

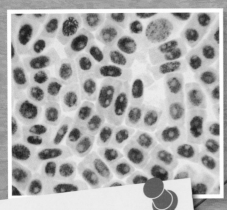

1935

Dutch scientist Frits Zernike invents the phase-contrast microscope. It lets investigators look at the parts of blood cells.

1966

British scientist Brian Culliford finds that blood protein is unique to an individual.

1984

Alec Jeffreys at the University of Leicester in England finds the first "genetic fingerprint" in blood.

1987

In Great Britain, DNA testing leads to the arrest of Colin Pitchfork for the murders of two girls.

1992

The Innocence Project is founded at the Benjamin N. Cardozo School of Law in New York. The organization works to free the wrongly convicted through DNA testing.

1996

In the United States, the DNA Databank goes into operation. This is a national collection of DNA samples from certain criminals.

2012

In New York, the DNA Databank is expanded. It now collects samples from all offenders.

Crime and DNA

In 1898, two girls were killed in Germany. Police suspected a man named Ludwig Tessnow. He had been seen near the girls and had stains on his clothes that looked like blood. Tessnow said they were wood dyes, and the police could not prove him wrong. Then, in 1901, two boys were found dead. This time, police had science on their side. They asked Paul Uhlenhuth to do his precipitin test. He found human blood on the clothes. Tessnow was found guilty in 1904. Blood testing was soon being used by many police forces in Europe. Not long after, this test spreads to other parts of the world.

Before blood testing, many people may have gotten away with murder by convincing police that the human bloodstains on their clothes were from paint, or from animal blood that got there during the butchering process.

In 1987, Europe again led the way. Two girls had been killed near Enderby, England. Using the new discoveries by British scientists, British police did a mass DNA screening of area men. The tests led to the arrest of a local baker, Colin Pitchfork. Pitchfork confessed. Meanwhile, in Chicago, Gary Dotson was still waiting for his name to be cleared. Around this same time, Gary Dotson was still waiting for his name to be cleared in Chicago. He was the man who had been accused of attacking Cathleen Crowell. He had not done it, but he could not prove it. Writer Sharon Begley heard about the Pitchfork case. She wrote about it in the magazine *Newsweek*. She called her article "Leaving Holmes in the Dust." Luckily for Dotson, his lawyer picked up a copy.

SHERLOCK HOLMES

In 1890, British writer Arthur Conan Doyle published the mystery *A Study in Scarlet*. The star of the book is Detective Sherlock Holmes. Holmes is known for his clever use of forensics. He uses a magnifying glass to look at tiny clues. He tests blood for poisons. He uses logic to put all the clues together to solve crimes. Doyle wrote a total of 60 stories about Holmes. Today, Holmes and his assistant Watson are two of the most famous fictional detectives in the world. Holmes shows up in TV programs, movies, and video games. We even use "Sherlock" to refer to people who are good at solving problems or mysteries.

DNA Today

In the 1980s, lawyers Peter Neufeld and Barry Scheck heard about DNA. It was all over the news. The two men liked what they heard. In 1992, they began the Innocence Project. Their goal was to get innocent people out of jail. They wanted to save people on **death row**. In many cases, they pushed for DNA tests. Since its start, the project has helped to free more than 300 people. They have also found more than 100 real offenders.

DNA is not only used to find the guilty. It also helps identify the dead. In the past, an explosion might not leave many clues. Now, bits of bone can be tested. DNA has even been used to identify the bones of soldiers from past wars. Other blood tests are still **vital** as well. Tests might be run after a car wreck. Maybe a driver was drunk. If so, he or she might be guilty of a crime. The uniqueness of DNA also makes it popular in court. While many types of evidence are used in a trial, DNA testing is the star.

DID YOU KNOW?

On August 23, 2016, Anthony Wright was released after serving 25 years in jail for a murder in Philadelphia. DNA evidence proved Wright's innocence, and pointed to a man named Ronnie Byrd.

death row: the area of a prison that houses prisoners who have been sentenced to death

vital: very important or necessary

At the Landstuhl Regional Medical Center in Landstuhl, Germany, the remains of American soldiers are kept until they are identified.

THE CSI EFFECT

CRIME SCENE DO NOT CROS...

Many crime shows begin with the discovery of a body but no witnesses to the crime.

Introduction

Many people love to learn about crimes. Detectives have been on TV since the 1940s. Before that, they were in books, radio, and films. These fictional detectives used the tools of crime scene investigation, or CSI. They looked for and "read" clues to get an idea of what happened. They decided who they should be looking for.

In the 1990s, these shows went high-tech. They showed off new forensic science. In 2000, the show *CSI: Crime Scene Investigation* had flashy labs and equipment. Some of it was made up for the show. The characters on the show made dazzling discoveries. They solved crimes in **mere** minutes. In 2002, Jeffrey Kluger wrote about the "CSI effect." He said that viewers expected real police and lawyers to do the same tricks. People liked to see physical clues. They did not like cases without DNA evidence. They began bringing those expectations to the **jury** box.

Some scientists say that shows like *CSI* create the false impression that forensic science never fails.

DID YOU KNOW?

In 1841, American writer Edgar Allan Poe wrote the first detective story, "The Murders in the Rue Morgue."

mere: the smallest or slightest amount

jury: a group of people who are chosen to make the decision in a legal case

The public took a special interest in the death of Caylee Anthony, setting up memorials near the spot where her body was found.

Forensics in Action

In July of 2008, the parents of a young woman in Florida were suspicious. They had not seen their daughter, Casey Anthony, for a month. They had also not seen Casey's daughter, Caylee. Finally, they asked for answers. Where was Caylee? Why did Casey's car smell like a dead body? Casey told many lies. She said the child was taken by a babysitter. But she did not even know the woman she named. Months later, the child's bones were found. Examiners could not tell a cause of death. There were no fingerprints or DNA to link to Casey. But she was charged with Caylee's death.

In May 2011, Casey went on trial. Her defense said her daughter had drowned in a pool. They said it was an accident. The prosecution said it was murder. Legal experts like Cyril Wecht felt their case was strong. But after only two days, Casey was found not guilty. One of the jurors said the lack of blood or DNA was a factor. Wecht was surprised. He says the CSI effect was at play. He says that in most cases, investigators do not know every detail of a crime. Shows like *CSI* may give juries the wrong idea. They may think that science should be able to prove guilt or innocence on its own. But in reality, juries must pay close attention to testimony, and fill in the blanks themselves.

DID YOU KNOW?

Hair is a good source of DNA, but only in the root—the part that is attached to the head. A hair that has broken off, instead of being pulled out of the head, does not contain DNA.

testimony: evidence given in court by witnesses or experts

Physical evidence in the trial included hair that might have been Caylee's, found in the trunk of her mother's car.

History of Forensics

How has the CSI effect evolved over time? Will it continue to impact crime solving?

1990

The show *Law & Order* debuts on NBC. It shows fictionalized crimes based on real ones, and focuses on evidence gathered by the police and presented in court.

1996

The documentary *Forensic Files* begins showing on the cable network TLC. It shows how real crimes were solved with forensic science. The tagline is "No witnesses. No leads. No problem."

1999

West Virginia University graduates only four students in forensic science.

2000

CSI goes on the air on the network station CBS. It shows high-tech equipment and techniques.

2004

Forensic science is now one of the most popular majors at West Virginia University. Four hundred students are enrolled in the program.

2005

In the trial of the actor Robert Blake, two men claim Blake asked them to kill his wife. Blake is found not guilty because of a lack of physical evidence. The Los Angeles district attorney publicly calls the jury "incredibly stupid."

2006

Professors at Eastern Michigan University survey 1,000 jurors. They claim to find no direct link between the watching of crime investigation shows and a need for forensic evidence in order to make a conviction.

2006

CSI is the second-most watched show according to Nielsen ratings. The show averages 25.2 million viewers per week.

2012

The American Bar Association puts out a set of instructions to lawyers for how to manage the CSI effect in jurors.

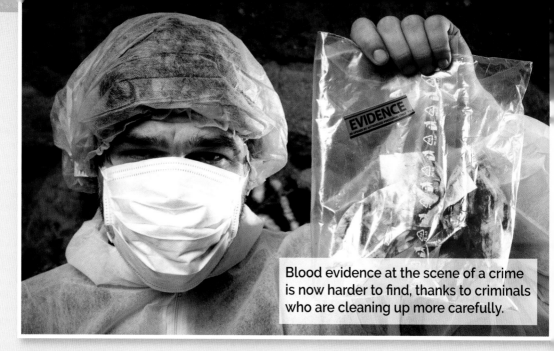

Blood evidence at the scene of a crime is now harder to find, thanks to criminals who are cleaning up more carefully.

Crime and the CSI Effect

Do verdicts come in "not guilty" more often since *CSI* began? Experts do not agree if the CSI effect sways juries or not. But most say it has changed the way police and lawyers act. Lawyers ask for as many physical clues as possible. The defense makes note of each missing link. Prosecutors avoid cases in which there are no such links. Some cases go untried, as prosecutors avoid cases that do not have physical evidence. They know these cases are hard to win. In court, defense teams will point out each piece of evidence the prosecution does not have. Before a trial, possible jurors are asked about what TV shows they watch. Lawyers also go high-tech in court. They might use a computer **simulation** of a crime. They hope this will wow a jury more than playing out the action or showing the jury a drawing.

simulation: a copy or demonstration of an act or process

The CSI effect may also change what crime looks like. Some police say criminals are now more careful. They clean up blood with bleach. Maybe they saw on TV that bleach gets rid of DNA. They tape envelopes shut because spit has DNA in it. They wear gloves. Criminals also seem to be "staging" scenes to throw police off track. They hide or destroy bodies. They hope the dead will not be found or identified. Juries have a hard time convicting someone of murder if there is no body.

Because of the CSI effect, investigators are now under more pressure to find clues. They spend more time than ever searching the scene of a crime.

DURST TRIAL

In 2003, Robert Durst was tried for murder in Texas. Police said he killed a man named Morris Black. Black's body was found with the head cut off, but his head was never found. Durst claimed self-defense. His lawyers said that if the head had been found, its wounds would have backed up Durst's claim. Robert Hirschhorn was a jury consultant for the defense. He found jurors who watched shows like *CSI*. He counted on these people to see the lack of the head as a vital gap in the evidence. He was right. Hurst was found not guilty.

The CSI Effect Today

If the CSI effect is real, is it a good or bad thing? If crooks cover their tracks, they might go free. Police feel pushed to find more clues. They do more tests. This should result in better work. But while the police work to find more clues, suspects' arrests are often delayed. As a result, they might commit more crimes.

Also, these tests are expensive. Police departments are not rich. Often, it is hard to fund a good crime lab. An under-funded lab can result in sloppy work and false results. An innocent person might go to jail.

There is also a plus side. Shows like *CSI* have boosted public interest in science. People are also more interested in the justice system. More students are studying forensics. There is more talent in the field. This is especially true for women and girls. They are inspired by the female scientists on shows like *Bones*. Some police forces also hope that the public's interest will help them. Maybe people will vote to give the police more tax dollars. Then they would be able to afford **cutting-edge** tools and experts, just like on TV.

cutting-edge: the most advanced

Many crime scene investigators start out by studying sciences like biology and chemistry in school.

Conclusion

What's next for forensics? As they did in the past, scientists today look for new ways to fight crime with science. A new camera can spot even tiny spots of blood. A new X-ray can do the same with fibers. Scientists also look for better ways to lift prints. Some of the chemicals used now are toxic. They are also very expensive. But researchers in Great Britain have found that an inexpensive spice, turmeric, works just as well. It highlights prints in yellow. And that is not all. Turmeric can also find traces of drugs.

Interest in forensic science is still on the rise. That means more students and more experts. That means more studies and more discoveries. Who knows what kinds of methods we will be talking about tomorrow?

Glossary

club foot: a foot that is misshapen and twisted out of its natural position

cold case: a crime that has been left unsolved for a long time

compromise: to reduce in value or usefulness

coroner: an official whose job is to find the cause of death when people die in sudden, violent, or suspicious ways

cutting-edge: the most advanced

death row: the area of a prison that houses prisoners who have been sentenced to death

defile: to dishonor or to make something impure

degrade: when something's properties or parts break down or wear away

forensics: the results of a scientific test done to help solve a crime

forge: to illegally create or change a document

foul play: criminal violence, murder, or dishonest acts

grisly: something that inspires disgust and fear

jury: a group of people who are chosen to make the decision in a legal case

mere: the smallest or slightest amount

morgue: a place where bodies are kept before being identified or buried

mug book: a police file of "mug shots," or photos taken of people who have been arrested

mummify: to preserve a body and wrap it in cloth

petty: small or not very important

prosecutor: the lawyer who is responsible for making a case against a person who has been charged with a crime

ruse: a trick or lie used to get someone to do something

Scotland Yard: the headquarters of the London police force

serial killer: someone who murders three or more people over a period of time, with breaks between the killings

simulation: a copy or demonstration of an act or process

taboo: something that a culture or society bans or avoids

testimony: evidence given in court by witnesses or experts

transfer: to pass from one person, place, or thing to another

tread: the impressed pattern left from the shoe of a person walking or a tire rolling over the ground

vital: very important or necessary

whorl: a pattern in the shape of a circle or a swirl around a central point

Quiz

1 Which celebrity death was called into question because the autopsy report doesn't match the body?

2 Through a CT scan scientists learned that King Tut had a club foot and which kind of disease?

3 Who created the first fingerprint ID system for use in crime fighting?

4 Which year was a test created to tell if blood came from a human or animal?

5 What's the name of the fictional detective known for his clever use of forensics?

6 To preserve a shoe or tire print in the snow, what is it sprayed with?

7 Which year did *CSI: Crime Scene Investigation* go on the air?

8 In 2004, how many errors were found in DNA tests in one Washington state lab?

8. 23

7. 2000

6. Wax

5. Sherlock Holmes

4. 1900

3. Juan Vucetich

2. A bone disease

1. John Dillinger

Index

Selected Bibliography

Beavan, Colin. *Fingerprints: The Origins of Crime Detection and the Murder Case That Launched Forensic Science.* New York: Hyperion, 2001.

Engdahl, Sylvia. *Forensic Technology.* Detroit, Mich.: Greenhaven Press, 2011.

Platt, Richard. *Crime Scene: The Ultimate Guide to Forensic Science.* New York: DK Publishing, 2003.

Wecht, Cyril H. *From Crime Scene to Courtroom: Examining the Mysteries Behind Famous Cases.* Amherst, N.Y.: Prometheus Books, 2011.

"Forensic Science History." New York: New York State Police, n.d. Web. Accessed February 6, 2017. https://www.troopers.ny.gov/Crime_Laboratory_System/History/Forensic_Science_History/.

U.S. Department of Justice. "Next Generation Identification (NGI)." Washington, D.C.: Federal Bureau of Investigation, n.d. Web. Accessed February 6, 2017. https://www.fbi.gov/services/cjis/fingerprints-and-other-biometrics/ngi/.

"Blood Typing and Types of Modern Day Forensics." New Orleans, LA: Loyola University New Orleans, n.d. Web. Accessed February 6, 2017. http://elearning.loyno.edu/masters-nursing-degree-online/resource/modern-forensics/.

Dysart, Katie L. "Managing the CSI Effect in Jurors." American Bar Association. American Bar Association, May 28, 2012. Web. Accessed February 6, 2017. https://apps.americanbar.org/litigation/committees/trialevidence/articles/winterspring2012-0512-csi-effect-jurors.html.

HOW DID IT HAPPEN?

WORLD WAR I

R.G. Grant

LUCENT BOOKS
An imprint of Thomson Gale, a part of The Thomson Corporation

THOMSON
™
GALE

Detroit • New York • San Francisco • San Diego • New Haven, Conn.
Waterville, Maine • London • Munich

Produced by Arcturus Publishing Ltd
26/27 Bickels Yard
151–153 Bermondsey Street
London SE1 3HA

© 2005 Arcturus Publishing

Series concept: Alex Woolf
Editor: Rebecca Gerlings
Designer: Stonecastle Graphics
Picture researcher: Thomas Mitchell

Cover Photo: CORBIS Rights Managed
Picture credits:
All images copyright of Getty Images

For more information, contact
Lucent Books
27500 Drake Rd.
Farmington Hills, MI 48331-3535
Or you can visit our Internet site at http://www.gale.com

LIBRARY OF CONGRESS CATALOGING-IN-PUBLICATION DATA

    Grant, R.G.
      World War I / by Reg Grant.
        p. cm. — (How did it happen?)
      Includes bibliographical references and index.
      ISBN 1-59018-605-2 (hardcover : alk. paper)
      1. World War, 1914–1918—Juvenile literature. 2.
    World War, 1914–1918—Chronology—Juvenile
    literature. I. Title. II. Series.
    D521.G693 2005
    940.3—dc22
                                    2004024459

Printed in Singapore

Contents

1 The Origins of the War

In 1914, the major powers of Europe—Britain, Germany, France, Austria-Hungary, and Russia—had been at peace for more than forty years. But it was an armed peace. All the major powers sought to achieve security by having bigger armies and better armaments than their rivals. On the European mainland, countries imposed compulsory military service on their male population and were prepared to mobilize armies of millions of men in days. Peace was maintained only by the threat of war.

The last war between two of the major powers had occurred in 1870–1871, when the Germans, led by the king of Prussia, defeated France, annexing the French provinces of Alsace and Lorraine. As a result of this victory, the powerful German Empire was created, with the Prussian king as its emperor, or kaiser. The defeat of 1871 left France with a fear of German military might and a strong desire to recover Alsace-Lorraine. In 1894, the French Republic formed an alliance with the Russian Empire, which also feared German power and had conflicts with Germany's ally, the Hapsburg-ruled Austro-Hungarian Empire. The tension between the Franco-Russian alliance and the Central powers—Germany and Austria-Hungary—became a fixed feature of European international relations.

Britain stood aside from European alliances, relying on its powerful navy to make it secure from invasion. But during the early

Launched in 1906, the British battleship HMS Dreadnought had the most powerful guns of any warship in the world. The building of Dreadnought and other battleships of its class was part of a naval arms race between Britain and Germany.

VOICES FROM THE PAST

Dangerous arms race

In 1899 Tsar Nicholas II, the ruler of Russia, warned that the arms race in Europe—the constant struggle to produce larger armies, heavier guns, and bigger warships—would one day lead to war instead of preserving peace:

"The accelerating arms race is transforming the armed peace into a crushing burden that weighs on all nations, and if prolonged, will lead to the very cataclysm it seeks to avert."

John Keegan, *The First World War* (Hutchinson, 1998)

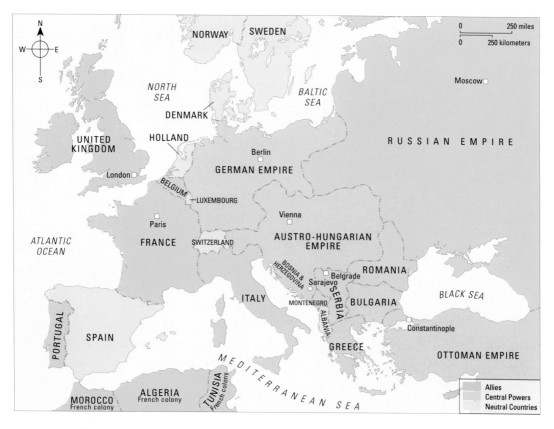

years of the twentieth century, the British became increasingly worried about the rising power of Germany. In 1900, the Germans embarked on a program of warship building that challenged British supremacy at sea. The British responded by engaging in a naval arms race with Germany. Also, in 1904, Britain negotiated an entente cordiale with France—an informal agreement on issues that might cause tension between the two countries. Britain did not sign an alliance, but over the following decade, British and French military leaders did form plans to resist a possible German attack.

Both Britain and France ruled large colonial empires in Africa and Asia. Germany, however, despite the power of its economy and military forces, had only a small overseas empire. This was a source of discontent for the Germans. Germany's efforts to expand its influence outside Europe threatened British and French interests. For example, in 1905 and again in 1911, Germany tried to contest French influence in Morocco. These confrontations were ultimately settled by compromise, but in 1911 in particular, they brought Europe to the very brink of war.

France reacted to what it saw as threats from Germany by introducing radical plans in 1913 to expand the size of its conscript

Before the war, the major confrontation in Europe was between the Central powers, or German and Austro-Hungarian empires, and France and the Russian Empire. After war broke out, the United Kingdom joined the side of France and Russia, and Belgium and Serbia were invaded by the Central powers.

army. Russia was also growing in military strength. To German leaders, who complained of "encirclement" by Russia and France, it seemed that their potential enemies were growing dangerously stronger.

The fatal crisis eventually came in the Balkans. Here, two wars involving Balkan states and the Ottoman Empire were fought in 1912–1913. They resulted in a great increase in the power and territory of Serbia. As Slavs, the Serbs were supported by Russia, the leading Slav power. But their increasing strength was deeply worrying to Austria-Hungary, which had a large Slav minority among its multinational population and had annexed Bosnia and Herzegovina—provinces with a substantial Serb population—in 1908.

Rush to War

When the Austrian archduke Franz Ferdinand—heir to the Austro-Hungarian throne—was shot by a Serb nationalist during a visit to Bosnia on June 28, 1914, key Austro-Hungarian military and political leaders were eager to make the assassination the pretext for declaring war on Serbia. They believed that a military victory over the upstart Slav state would strengthen the Hapsburg Empire. The Austrian emperor, Franz Josef, was more cautious. He insisted on consulting his German allies. The German emperor, Kaiser Wilhelm II, assured Austria-Hungary that it could "rely on Germany's full support."

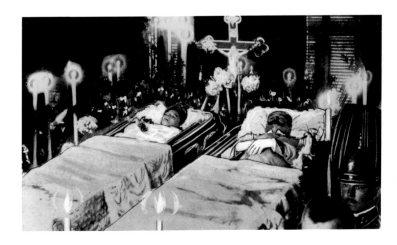

The bodies of Archduke Franz Ferdinand, heir to the throne of Austria-Hungary, and his wife are displayed after their assassination in Sarajevo. The killings, carried out by a Bosnian Serb, gave the Austro-Hungarian government an excuse for declaring war on Serbia.

Europe's leaders were slow to appreciate the seriousness of the situation. The kaiser left for his summer yachting holiday as planned. It was almost a month after the assassination before the Austro-Hungarian government made its move. On July 23, it sent an ultimatum to the Serbian government, threatening to declare war unless a series of humiliating demands were met. The Serbs agreed to

TURNING POINT

Assassination in Sarajevo

On June 28, 1914, Archduke Franz Ferdinand, heir to the throne of Austria-Hungary, visited Sarajevo, in the province of Bosnia. Among the crowds gathered to see the archduke were six young Bosnians who intended to kill him. They wanted to free Bosnia from Austro-Hungarian rule and make it part of Serbia instead. Their first attempt to kill the archduke with a bomb failed. But later in the day, by chance, the archduke's car stopped near a shop where one of the young Bosnians, nineteen-year-old Gavrilo Princip, had gone to buy a sandwich. He pulled out a gun and shot the archduke and his wife. Their deaths were the spark that ignited the First World War.

most of the demands but not all. Austria-Hungary declared war on Serbia on July 28. Russia meanwhile put its army on a war footing in readiness to support the Serbs.

The Austro-Hungarian declaration of war on Serbia led with breathtaking speed to a general European war. All countries' war plans were based on moving massive numbers of troops to the border by train and throwing them into the attack as quickly as possible. All feared that the enemy would get an attack in first, before they had time to complete the complicated process of mobilization. Germany felt itself in an especially difficult situation, because it expected to have to fight a war on two fronts—against Russia in the east and France in the west. Germany's war plan, the Schlieffen Plan, was based on achieving a rapid victory over France before the massive but inefficient Russian Army could get into action. This seemed to the German generals their only hope of success.

Once the Russians began to mobilize their troops, the German generals felt they must put the Schlieffen Plan into immediate effect, even though Russia's intention was only to oppose an Austro-Hungarian attack on Serbia. The kaiser contacted his cousin, Tsar Nicholas II of Russia, on July 29 with an appeal for peace, to which the tsar responded positively. But General Helmuth von Moltke, head of the German general staff, in effect overruled his emperor, arguing that to interrupt war preparations would leave Germany exposed to a Russian invasion.

Future enemies, Tsar Nicholas II of Russia (left) and Germany's Kaiser Wilhelm II (right) ride side by side in a royal carriage about two years before the war. All the royal heads of state in Europe were closely related. For example, Kaiser Wilhelm was cousin to both Tsar Nicholas and Britain's King George V.

Conflicting emotions

A British soldier described the mixed emotions of crowds watching him and his colleagues leave for the war at the port of Felixstowe in August 1914:

> "[People were] cheering, shouting, singing, waving their handkerchiefs. . . . Some of the young girls were even pelting us with flowers. . . . I turned up my head and found myself inches from a woman who was staring into my face. . . . As I went by I could see that she had tears in her eyes."

Lyn Macdonald, *1914: The Days of Hope* (Penguin, 1989)

Civilians who have volunteered to join the British Army shortly after the outbreak of the war are escorted through the streets by soldiers in uniform. In the autumn of 1914, the British Army received about 30,000 new recruits every day.

On August 1, Germany declared war on Russia after the Russians refused to halt mobilization. Two days later, Germany declared war on France, having failed to obtain a promise from the French to keep out of the war. Whether Britain would enter the conflict was at that point still uncertain. Some British leaders felt that

HOW DID IT HAPPEN?

Was Germany responsible for starting the war?

Some historians have argued that Germany started the First World War in order to achieve military domination of Europe. Immanuel Geiss wrote: "Germany was the aggressor . . . deliberately provoking Russia. This drove Russia, France and Britain . . . into a position where they could not but react against massive German ambitions." Others have agreed that Germany played the leading part in starting the war, but because of fears for its own security. The German leaders, it is argued, feared the growing power of Russia and decided it was best to fight in 1914, while they still had a chance of victory, rather than later, when they would lose.

Many historians, however, hold that Europe slipped into war more or less by accident and that Germany deserves no special blame. Military historian Richard Holmes, for example, wrote that Europe's "political and military leaders were wrestling with problems quite beyond their resources" and that the events leading up to the war were a "calamity" that no one could control.

Niall Ferguson, *The Pity of War* (Penguin, 1998); Richard Holmes, *The Western Front* (BBC, 1999)

Britain must go to war in support of France to maintain a balance of power in Europe. They believed that if Germany dominated the European mainland, this would be a threat to British independence. Others believed Britain should stay out of a continental war. The issue was settled, however, when Germany invaded neutral Belgium on August 4—a necessary part of implementing the Schlieffen Plan. Britain had guaranteed Belgium's neutrality and declared war on Germany in its defense.

In going to war, governments enjoyed the overwhelming support of their people. Cheering, flag-waving crowds filled the centers of major cities across Europe, and where they were not forced into armies by conscription, thousands of men rushed to volunteer to fight. Of course, many people also felt dismayed and fearful at the prospect of a general war. But in all combatant countries, on both sides of the conflict, the vast majority of people believed that the war was being fought for a just cause and in self-defense.

2 Not Over by Christmas

In August 1914, some 6 million men were mobilized for war on the European continent. Field Marshal Lord Horatio Herbert Kitchener, made British secretary of state for war at the start of the conflict, told the British government that the war would probably last from three to four years. But this was not what most people expected. The general belief was that the war would be decided quickly by a series of immensely destructive but rapidly fought battles. It would be "all over by Christmas."

At first it seemed there might indeed be a quick end to the conflict. Within less than a month of the war's starting, Germany appeared to have victory within its grasp. Implementing the Schlieffen Plan, the Germans concentrated the major part of their forces on an offensive through Belgium. The small Belgian Army resisted gallantly, slowing the Germans' progress, but the invaders soon broke through and advanced toward the French border. On the way, German soldiers burned down some villages and towns and executed groups of civilians suspected of acts of resistance. These atrocities in Belgium turned many people who were neutral, especially in the United States, against Germany.

German soldiers march through the Belgian capital, Brussels, in August 1914. Germany's invasion of neutral Belgium and its sometimes brutal behavior toward the Belgian people shocked the world.

Meanwhile, in mid-August, the French Army began an offensive in Lorraine, intending to break through the German defenses and surge into Germany. The offensive was a catastrophe. The French infantry and cavalry, in their bright blue uniforms, launched themselves in mass attacks upon German fortified positions. They were massacred by machine guns, rapid rifle fire, and artillery. The French lost hundreds of thousands of troops in this Battle of the Frontiers and were driven back in disarray.

By August 20, British troops shipped across the English Channel had taken up a position on the extreme left of the French line. The British Expeditionary Force (BEF) was small by continental standards—a little over 100,000 men—because Britain did not have compulsory military service, depending instead on a small professional army. The BEF found itself directly in the path of the far more powerful German forces advancing through Belgium. On August 24, the British troops encountered the advancing Germans at Mons. After putting up valiant resistance, the BEF was forced to withdraw. With their French allies, the British retreated through the rest of August, falling back toward Paris.

While the Germans looked triumphant on the Western Front, they seemed in trouble in the east. The basis of German strategy was the hope that victory in the west could be achieved before the Russian

Members of the British Expeditionary Force (BEF), along with Belgian soldiers, retreat after the Battle of Mons. Although fighting valiantly, the BEF and the Belgians were unable to hold their positions in the face of the overwhelming power of the German onslaught.

VOICES FROM THE PAST

The shock of war

Charles de Gaulle, a future president of France, was a captain in the French Army in 1914. He described the shock felt by French troops—brought up to believe that bravery was the key to victory in war—when they first encountered German firepower:

"Suddenly the enemy's fire became precise and concentrated. Second by second the hail of bullets and the thunder of shells grew stronger. Those who survived lay flat on the ground, amid the screaming wounded and the humble corpses. . . . In an instant it had become clear that not all the courage in the world could withstand this fire."

Richard Holmes, *The Western Front* (BBC, 1999)

forces could mount a serious attack on Germany. But the Russians mobilized far faster and more effectively than the Germans had thought possible. By August 17, Russian armies were advancing into German territory in East Prussia. The Germans responded to this crisis by appointing Field Marshal Paul von Hindenburg to command the Eastern Front, with General Erich Ludendorff as his chief of staff. They also transferred some troops from the Western Front to strengthen their forces in the east.

German Field Marshal Paul von Hindenburg (center), and his chief of staff, General Erich Ludendorff (right), became national heroes in Germany after their victory over the Russians at Tannenberg in August 1914.

Victory in the East

The Germans were heavily outnumbered by the Russians in East Prussia but, by skillful maneuvering, Hindenburg and Ludendorff achieved a devastating victory during the Battle of Tannenberg fought on August 26–31. Around 100,000 Russian troops were taken prisoner, and about 50,000 were killed or wounded. The Russian commander, General Alexander Samsonov, committed suicide. The Germans went on to drive Russian forces out of East Prussia, decisively ending the threat of an invasion of Germany from the east.

Far less satisfactory, from a German point of view, was the performance of its ally Austria-Hungary. The first attempt by the Austro-Hungarian Army to invade Serbia—the almost forgotten

TURNING POINT

The taxis of the Marne

On September 3, 1914, General Joseph Galliéni, commander of French troops in Paris, was anxiously preparing to defend the city against the advancing German First Army. He learned by reports from reconnaissance aircraft, however, that the Germans had turned southward to pass east of Paris. The following day, Galliéni launched a bold attack on the flank of the German Army near the River Marne. It was a desperate venture. At one point, lacking transport, troops were rushed from Paris to the battlefield in taxis. But the surprise attack turned the tide of the war. Other Allied troops also counterattacked and forced the Germans to retreat. Paris was saved.

French soldiers prepare to use a captured German machine gun during the Battle of the Marne in September 1914. One of the main difficulties the Allied troops had at this stage of the war was a desperate shortage of machine guns of their own.

pretext for the whole conflict—proved a costly failure. Battle hardened through their experience in the Balkan Wars, the Serb troops were more than a match for the invaders. In Galicia, clashes between Austro-Hungarian and Russian forces soon went in favor of the Russians, who captured the city of Lemberg (or L'viv) in early September. Germany was forced to transfer troops southward from East Prussia to support the Austro-Hungarians.

Meanwhile, on the Western Front, the run of German successes came to an end in the first week of September. According to the Schlieffen Plan, the German armies sweeping down from Belgium were supposed to advance behind the French armies facing the German border. The French would be encircled and destroyed. But the German victory in Lorraine had driven the French back from the frontier zone, making encirclement more difficult. Also, the long march through Belgium and northern France had exhausted German troops and stretched their lines of supply—all supplies having to be carried by horse-drawn vehicles. The Germans swung to the east of Paris, instead of to the west of the city as originally planned, partly to reduce the distance they had to travel. East of Paris, the French and British counterattacked at the Battle of the Marne.

On September 9, the German high command ordered its forces to retreat northward. The Allies set off in pursuit, scenting a chance of victory. When the Germans reached the Aisne River, however, they dug trenches and held their ground. The British and French were incapable of breaking through this defensive position.

Race to the Sea

There was still a large area of open country between the Aisne and the Channel coast that was under no one's control. From September through November, the Germans and the Allies made a series of attempts to outflank one another in this area, drawing ever closer to the coast. This "Race to the Sea" resulted in a number of extremely costly battles as each successive outflanking move was blocked. The last of these battles, occurring near the Belgian town of Ypres (or Ieper) from October 19 to November 22, is estimated to have cost a quarter of a million British, French, and German casualties.

Cavalry from Algeria (then a French colony) take a rest after fighting at the Battle of the Aisne in September 1914. Soldiers from Africa and Asia played an important part in the conflict.

From mid-November, the onset of winter brought an end to the war of movement. The two sides dug themselves into trenches, facing one another along a front line that stretched unbroken from the English Channel in the north to the border of neutral Switzerland in

the south. On the Eastern Front a stable, if looser, line was held as Christmas approached. The human cost of the fighting in 1914 had been unprecedented. France and Germany combined were grieving for over half a million young men killed. Around a third of the British troops sent to France in August had died. Russia and Austria-Hungary had each lost well over a million soldiers who were dead, wounded, or taken prisoner. Yet the fighting had had no decisive result, except to prove how difficult it was going to be for either side to achieve victory.

All armies in the First World War depended heavily on horse-drawn vehicles. This is one reason why decisive, rapid offensives were so hard to carry out. Here, the Bulgarian Army prepares to move up the front line in October 1915.

HOW DID IT HAPPEN?

Could Germany have won the war in 1914?

People have long debated whether, by implementing the original Schlieffen Plan properly, the Germans could have defeated France in August to September 1914. The plan called for German strength to be concentrated on the advance down from Belgium, which was intended to encircle and destroy the French. But the German commander, Field Marshal Helmuth von Moltke, weakened these forces, especially by transferring two corps to fight Russia on the Eastern Front.

It has been questioned, however, whether the Schlieffen Plan could ever have succeeded. It required German troops to advance on foot twenty-five miles a day and fight at the end of ever-lengthening supply lines. Under any circumstances, the exhausted Germans would have become increasingly vulnerable to a counterattack.

3 Stalemate

The fighting of 1914 left Germany in possession of part of northern France—a valuable area with many factories and mines—and most of Belgium. Britain and France began 1915 determined to drive the Germans out of this territory. But when they attempted renewed large-scale offensives, they found they could make no progress. Battles such as Neuve Chapelle in March 1915 and Loos in September produced nothing but heavy casualties.

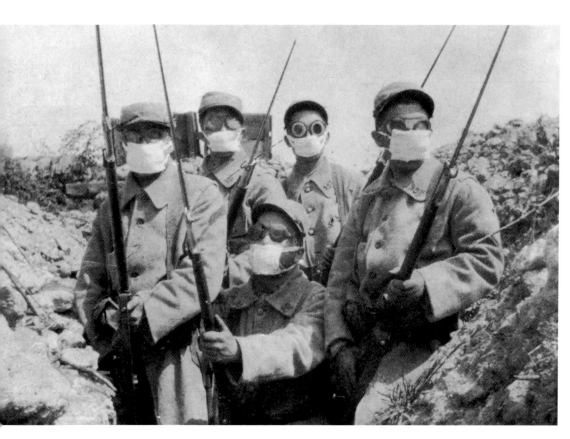

French soldiers in trenches in 1915 wear an early form of gas mask. Goggles cover their eyes and pads soaked in protective chemicals cover their mouths.

The front line from the English Channel to Switzerland remained unchanged throughout the year, except in minor detail.

The reason for the stalemate on the Western Front was the dominance of defense over attack. On both sides, armies dug systems of trenches to protect themselves against enemy fire. Barbed wire was set out in front of the trench. Attackers had to climb out of their trenches and cross no-man's-land under fire from accurate rifles, machine guns, and artillery. They then had to pass through the barbed

VOICES FROM THE PAST

Death by gassing

Poison gas was first used by the Germans at Ypres in April 1915. Six days after the first gas attack, the British general, John Charteris, wrote in his diary:

"The horrible part of it is the slow lingering death of those who are gassed. I saw some hundred poor fellows laid out in the open . . . slowly drowning with water in their lungs."

H.P. Willmott, *First World War* (Dorling Kindersley, 2003)

wire to occupy the enemy trench. The defenders would sometimes have a second trench behind the first, so the whole process then had to be repeated. Even if an attacking force managed a momentary breakthrough, it lacked the mobility to advance swiftly through the hole it had made, and the defenders were able to bring up reserves to plug the gap.

Artillery bombardment was used to soften up enemy defenses before an attack, but the shells had only limited effect against well-entrenched troops. At the Second Battle of Ypres in April 1915, the Germans made the first use of poison gas in an attempt to disrupt defenses, at first with some success. Gas was soon extensively used by the Allies as well, but the development of countermeasures such as gas masks quickly limited its effectiveness on either side. In the end, the resort to chemical warfare made the battlefield even more dangerous and fearful but had no decisive effect.

On the Eastern Front, warfare was more mobile than in the west, because there was always room to maneuver in the vast spaces over which armies operated. The Russians fared badly during 1915, retreating in the face of a combined German and Austro-Hungarian offensive in the summer. Yet there was no more immediate chance of a decisive victory in the east than in the west.

The combatant countries faced the prospect of a long conflict, in which success would require the massive commitment of industrial

With millions of working men enrolled in the army, Britain was forced to employ women in armaments factories. This sort of work was previously done exclusively by men and was exhausting and dangerous.

production and manpower. By the start of 1915, all the armies were already running short of munitions, especially artillery shells. Countries realized that they needed to organize their industries to maximum effect to support the war effort, while at the same time recruiting the largest possible number of men for the fighting. Britain held out for a long time against the need to introduce conscription. Around 2.5 million British citizens joined the army as volunteers in 1914–1916—almost as many as the army could accommodate. Britain could also draw on troops from its empire and dominions. Canada, Australia, New Zealand, and India in particular provided large forces of fighting men. But even in Britain, conscription was finally introduced in 1916.

Soldiers from the Indian subcontinent—then ruled by Britain—fought bravely on the Western Front in 1914 and 1915. They suffered heavy casualties and were withdrawn from Europe from 1915 onward.

Civilians rarely became the direct targets of military action, although a small number of air raids were carried out on cities as German zeppelins, or airships, attacked London from 1915 onward. But civilians were nonetheless profoundly affected by the war. To replace the millions of men being sent to the front, women were drawn into jobs formerly done exclusively by men—from driving buses to working in armaments factories. There were increasing shortages of essential goods, including staple foods, which led to hunger and unrest in many European cities.

Britain and France were better placed than their enemies for a long war, because they could import supplies by sea from around the world, including food and raw materials. The United States was an especially important supplier. Germany tried to cut off these supplies

TURNING POINT

Sinking of the *Lusitania*

On May 7, 1915, the ocean liner *Lusitania*, one of the world's largest and most luxurious passenger ships, was hit by a torpedo fired by a German submarine. The *Lusitania* sank in eighteen minutes, drowning more than 1,200 passengers and crew. The liner had been sailing from New York to Liverpool, and 128 of the drowned passengers were Americans. The Germans claimed that the liner had been carrying troops and war matériel but, in fact, it had only a small quantity of ammunition on board. The attack caused anti-German riots in Britain and outraged American public opinion. Shortly afterward, Germany had to scale down U-boat activity to avoid war with the United States.

German U-boats line up in Kiel Harbor during the First World War. The use of submarines to attack merchant ships ultimately played a major part in bringing the United States into the war against Germany.

by using submarines—the U-boats—to sink merchant ships bound for Britain. But the U-boat campaign had to be limited from mid-1915, after the United States threatened to enter the war if attacks on American ships continued.

The surface warships of Britain's Royal Navy, meanwhile, imposed a highly effective blockade that prevented food and raw materials for industry from being imported by the Central powers.

The rival navies of Britain and Germany fought only one major sea battle, at Jutland from May to June 1916. Although the Royal Navy lost more ships than the Germans lost, the battle confirmed British domination of the sea, and the German fleet never left port again in the course of the war.

As the war went on, more countries were drawn into the conflict. Italy joined the war on the Allied side in May 1915, after the Allies secretly agreed that the Italians could seize territory from Austria-Hungary if victory was won. In the summer of 1915, Bulgaria joined Germany and Austria-Hungary in an offensive in the Balkans that at last broke Serbian resistance. Serbia was occupied and the remnants of the Serbian Army escaped into exile.

Further afield, Japan declared war on Germany and took the opportunity to snap up German possessions in China and the Pacific. Germany's colonies in Africa were attacked by troops from the British dominion of South Africa.

Heavy artillery, such as this Italian howitzer, was used by all sides in the war to rain down massive quantities of explosives upon enemy trenches. This sort of heavy shelling, however, repeatedly failed to lead to any decisive breakthrough in trench warfare.

But by far the most important geographical widening of the conflict resulted from the Ottoman Empire (Turkey) entering the war on the German side in November 1914. Because the Turks ruled an area stretching from the Mediterranean to Mesopotamia, their entry into the war led to far-reaching consequences for the entire Middle East.

Faced with stalemate on the Western Front, in the spring of 1915, Britain decided to attempt to capture the Ottoman capital, Constantinople (Istanbul), thus opening up a sea route to provide military aid to Russia. A large military force, including many Australians and New Zealanders, landed on the Turkish coast at Gallipoli in April in order to seize control of the straits that led to Constantinople. But the troops met fierce resistance from the Turkish Army and some 250,000 men were killed or wounded before the operation was finally abandoned in January 1916.

HOW DID IT HAPPEN?

Why did men go on fighting?

Historians have debated why troops kept on fighting despite the terrible conditions under which the war was fought and heavy casualties. One obvious reason was what military historian Keith Simpson called "fear of the consequences of disobedience." For example, 346 British soldiers were executed for refusing to fight. There was also a strong sense of solidarity with comrades in arms—soldiers did not want to let their friends down. Patriotism was a further powerful motive—they felt it was their duty to win the war on their country's behalf. British war correspondent Philip Gibbs wrote of men on opposing sides being driven by "a deep and simple love of England [or] Germany."

But historian Niall Ferguson has asserted that an instinctive love of fighting and killing also played its part, writing: "Men kept fighting because they wanted to." He quotes a Canadian soldier who described the war as "the greatest adventure of my life. . . . I would not have missed it for anything."

Keith Simpson, quoted in Richard Holmes, *The Western Front* (BBC, 1999); Philip Gibbs, quoted in H.P. Willmott, *First World War* (Dorling Kindersley, 2003); Niall Ferguson, *The Pity of War* (Penguin, 1998)

An Australian soldier carries a wounded comrade during the fighting at Gallipoli in 1915. About 11,000 of the 48,000 Allied soldiers killed in the Gallipoli campaign were from Australia or New Zealand.

Elsewhere in the Ottoman Empire, the British fought the Turks with mixed success in Mesopotamia and supported a revolt against Turkish rule by Arabs in what is now Saudi Arabia—an operation in which T.E. Lawrence ("Lawrence of Arabia") played a significant part. For their part, the Turks invaded the Caucasia region of Russia in the winter of 1914–1915, only to be driven back with heavy losses. The worst consequence of the war with Russia was felt by the Armenians, more than 2 million of

whom lived under Turkish rule. Suspecting the Armenians of cooperating with the Russians, the Turkish government had the whole population deported. Around 1.5 million Armenians died of hardship and massacre between 1915 and 1917. Wherever the war spread its tentacles, it brought death and suffering on an awesome scale.

4 Near the Breaking Point

D espite the widening of the conflict to other parts of the world, the combatant countries remained certain that the war would be won or lost on the major battlefields of Europe. After a year of frustration in 1915, they prepared for even mightier offensives in 1916, ready to use the now much greater quantity of arms and ammunition being supplied by their war industries.

At a conference held at Chantilly, France, in December 1915, the British, French, Italians, and Russians agreed on a plan to mount simultaneous offensives so that the Central Powers would have to fight on all fronts at once. But the Germans had their own attacking plans. General Erich von Falkenhayn, who had taken over from Moltke as German chief of general staff, decided to concentrate his forces against the French fortress city of Verdun. He believed that the French would feel obliged to defend Verdun at any cost. It would become a killing ground on which, Falkenhayn wrote, "the forces of France will bleed to death."

VOICES FROM THE PAST

Annihilation

German soldiers suffered as heavily in the battles of 1916 as the British and French did. Lieutenant Ernst Jünger described the German lines in September 1916:

"The sunken road now appeared as nothing but a series of enormous shell-holes filled with pieces of uniform, weapons and dead bodies. . . . Among the living lay the dead. As we dug ourselves in we found them in layers stacked one on top of the other. One company after another had been shoved into the drum-fire [machine-gun fire] and steadily annihilated."

Ernst Jünger, *Storm of Steel* (Penguin, 2004)

The Germans launched their offensive against Verdun on February 21, 1916, with the heaviest artillery bombardment the world had yet seen. As Falkenhayn had guessed, the French government decreed that Verdun must be held at whatever cost. General Philippe Pétain was put in command of the defense of the city, and hundreds of thousands of French troops were funneled into that small sector of

the front. A single road, soon known to the French as the *voie sacrée* (sacred way), linked Verdun to the rear. Although the road was under continual artillery bombardment, around 3,000 trucks traveled along it every day, carrying men and supplies to the battlefield.

Falkenhayn had anticipated that the French troops would simply be worn down by artillery fire, keeping German casualties to a minimum. But the German troops were increasingly drawn into fierce combat, some of it at close quarters in and around the old forts that had been built to defend Verdun. By the time the offensive was called off in early June, the Germans had suffered over 280,000 casualties— only slightly less than the 315,000 French dead or wounded. And for all their efforts, the Germans still failed to take Verdun, allowing France to claim a victory.

At the Chantilly conference, the British and French had agreed to launch a joint offensive on the section of the Western Front near the

French troops crouch down as artillery shells explode in front of them during the Battle of Verdun in 1916. At the start of the battle, the German guns fired over a million shells in a single day.

Somme River in the summer of 1916. The French losses at Verdun so weakened France's army, however, that it had limited resources left to throw into a new offensive. The British Army, on the other hand, had been growing rapidly in size as volunteers joined up in the hundreds of thousands. So the Somme offensive became a largely British operation, under the command of Field Marshal Sir Douglas Haig.

British machine gunners in gas masks take part in the Battle of the Somme in 1916. The use of machine guns by both sides meant that troops advancing toward enemy trenches were mowed down in the thousands.

Haig believed that a prolonged artillery bombardment, backed up by the exploding of mines in tunnels dug under the German lines, would break German resistance. Infantry would advance to occupy the devastated German trenches, and cavalry would ride through into open country behind the German lines. But the disastrous first day of the battle, on July 1, proved the artillery was nowhere near as effective as Haig expected. The following months reinforced this lesson. Despite attack after attack by Allied infantry, the German lines barely moved. Beaumont-Hamel, for example, was one of the objectives that the British intended to seize on July 1; they actually took it on November 13, the day the offensive was finally called off.

TURNING POINT

First day of the Somme

On July 1, 1916, the British Army, along with a lesser number of French troops, launched a major offensive on the Somme. In the eight days before the offensive, over a million artillery shells were fired at the German trenches. This bombardment was expected to crush German resistance. British infantry— mostly new troops entering their first battle—were ordered to advance at walking pace across no-man's-land to occupy the German lines. But as the troops advanced, the Germans emerged unscathed from their deep shelters and opened fire. The shelling had also failed to clear away the barbed wire in front of the German trenches. Unable to advance, and caught in machine-gun fire, line after line of British soldiers were mowed down. Of 100,000 men who attacked that day, almost 20,000 were killed and another 40,000 were wounded or missing in action.

Around 600,000 Allied troops were killed or wounded in the Battle of the Somme. Estimates of German casualties vary, but they were almost certainly on a similar scale. Overshadowed by this immense slaughter were a few positive developments. A newly created British mass army began to find out how to fight—a painful and expensive learning process, but learning nonetheless. Also, new weapons were introduced that could potentially break the deadlock. The British used tanks for the first time at the Somme, although there were too few of them, and they were too slow and unreliable to have much effect. Aircraft had begun to play an important part in the war— employed chiefly as "eyes in the sky"—directing artillery fire on to enemy targets. But the planes were not yet very effective as bombers, or for attacking troops on the ground. For the time being, increasing supplies of arms and munitions simply increased the toll of dead and wounded.

The Pressure Mounts

On the Eastern Front, in 1916, there was once again more movement than in the west, but mass slaughter on a similar scale. In the spring, the Russians launched an offensive in Poland. Their troops outnumbered the Germans by six to one, yet the Russians were driven back with heavy losses. In June, however, the Russian general Alexei

Brusilov launched a successful offensive against Austro-Hungarian forces in Galicia. Attacking without a preparatory artillery bombardment, his troops took the Austro-Hungarians by surprise and drove them back in disarray, taking more than 300,000 prisoners. Germany was forced to transfer troops from the Western Front to counterattack the Russians. Despite the initial success, Russia eventually lost around a million men in the Brusilov offensive— killed, wounded, or taken prisoner—for little ultimate gain.

Battered by the Russian offensive, and also engaging the Italians in the south, the Austro-Hungarian Army was almost spent by the summer of 1916. Germany had to take command of its ally's military forces to keep them fighting. The effectiveness of this move was shown when Romania declared war on the Central powers in August 1916, hoping to take advantage of Austria-Hungary's weakness to seize territory from Hungary. Romania was soon invaded by armies under German command, and its capital, Bucharest, fell to the Central powers in December.

David Lloyd George (right), British prime minister from December 1916 to the end of the war, talks to French commander General Joseph Joffre (center) and British commander Field Marshal Sir Douglas Haig.

HOW DID IT HAPPEN?

Lions led by donkeys?

The troops in the trenches have been described as "lions led by donkeys"—courageous men sent to their deaths in futile offensives by generals who were insensitive, unimaginative fools. Historian A.J.P. Taylor summed up this view of the war as "brave helpless soldiers; blundering obstinate generals; nothing achieved."

But other historians have argued that the generals fought the war in the only way it could be fought, at a time when artillery, machine guns, and barbed wire dominated the battlefield. Historian John Keegan wrote: "The basic and stark fact . . . was that the conditions of warfare between 1914 and 1918 predisposed towards slaughter and that only an entirely different technology, one not available until a generation later, could have averted such an outcome."

A.J.P. Taylor, *The First World War* (Penguin, 1963); John Keegan, *The First World War* (Hutchinson, 1998)

General Alexei Brusilov was the most successful Russian general of the war, inflicting a severe setback upon Austria-Hungary with his offensive in the summer of 1916. But even Brusilov was not able to achieve a decisive victory and his offensive ultimately cost Russia many men.

The massive scale of losses at the front, and lack of prospect of an end to the war, put immense strain on people's loyalty to their governments. So did the mounting hardship among civilians, especially where food shortages became serious, as in Austria-Hungary and Russia. Austria-Hungary faced particular problems because the loyalty of the different nationalities within the empire weakened as the war went on. There were, for example, large-scale desertions by Czech troops from the Austro-Hungarian Army during 1916. Britain faced its own nationalist problem in Ireland, where Republicans seeking independence from British rule staged an uprising in Dublin on Easter 1916, hoping for German support that never came. The uprising was repressed by the British Army in a brutal manner that turned many more Irish people against British rule. In Russia, the tsarist regime had reached the breaking point by the end of the year and was on the brink of a revolution that would change the course of world history.

5 America Joins the War

By the end of 1916, the Central powers were pessimistic about the future of the war. The German government made an offer of peace to the Allies, based on Germany keeping possession of the territory it currently held—a proposal totally unacceptable to the Allied powers. After the peace offer had been rejected, Germany's leaders decided upon a desperate gamble. They would resume unlimited U-boat warfare, hoping to sink enough merchant ships to bring Britain to its knees. The Germans knew that the United States would probably enter the war if its merchant ships were sunk, but gambled that the war could be won before American manpower and industrial might could have any effect on the European battlefield.

Believing that the U-boats could win the war, the Germans decided to use a defensive strategy on the Western Front. In early 1917, German troops were withdrawn to newly constructed fortified positions along what was known as the Hindenburg Line. The Allies, by contrast, continued to have confidence in attack. A charismatic general, Robert Nivelle, took over from Joseph Joffre as French commander in chief and promised to "win the war in 48 hours" with a single, concentrated offensive. Launched in April 1917, the Nivelle offensive proved an utter disaster. The Allies lost around 350,000 men for almost no gain. In the wake of the offensive there were widespread mutinies in the French Army. Nivelle was dismissed and replaced by Pétain, who restored order in the ranks with a mixture of firmness and concessions. But the spirit of the French Army was broken.

French deserters make their way toward German lines to surrender to the enemy. From April to May 1917, many French soldiers refused to obey orders and organized protests against their officers. However, few actually deserted, and morale was gradually restored.

Allied offensives on the Western Front, with British and Commonwealth forces playing the leading role, continued through the year. The fighting at Ypres in July to November, which became known as the Battle of Passchendaele, was perhaps the most hellish of the war. Some soldiers simply drowned in the mud as constant rainfall

French soldiers captured by the Germans during the disastrous Nivelle offensive of spring 1917 are taken away to a prisoner-of-war camp. In general, prisoners-of-war on both sides of the Western Front were well treated.

VOICES FROM THE PAST

A call for peace

Siegfried Sassoon, a British poet and army officer with a record of exceptional bravery, decided in 1917 that the war must be ended. He issued a public appeal for peace:

"I believe that the war is being deliberately prolonged by those who have the power to end it. . . . I have seen and endured the suffering of the troops, and I can no longer be a party to prolong these sufferings for ends which I believe to be evil and unjust."

Sassoon's peace appeal was dismissed by the authorities as the product of shell shock, and he was sent to a military hospital.

Jon Stallworthy, *Wilfred Owen: A Biography* (OUP, 1975)

Canadian soldiers use shell holes to provide cover during the fighting at Passchendaele in 1917. The conditions at Passchendaele were terrible, with mud sometimes so deep that men who slipped into it sank without trace.

reduced the battlefield to a swamp. As usual, Allied advances of a few hundred yards were bought with tens of thousands of casualties. Meanwhile, in Italy, German and Austro-Hungarian forces managed a breakthrough at Caporetto in October, forcing Britain and France to transfer resources to the Italian front to prevent their ally from being defeated.

The Collapse of Russia

If 1917 was a year of continuing stalemate on the Western Front, on the Eastern Front it brought dramatic changes. In Russia, the tsarist regime collapsed under the strain of the war. Tsar Nicholas II was forced to abdicate in March after a popular uprising provoked by food shortages in the capital, Petrograd (or St. Petersburg). A provisional government took over, dedicated to continuing the war. The strongest figure in the new government was Alexander Kerensky. In the summer of 1917, Kerensky ordered a major offensive to drive the enemy from Russian soil. It proved a costly failure.

Meanwhile, antiwar feeling in Russia was mounting. Russian revolutionary Vladimir Ilyich Lenin, the leader of the Bolshevik Party, was in exile in Switzerland when the tsarist regime fell. In April, Lenin accepted a German offer of transport back to his homeland, crossing Germany in a sealed train. As the Germans had hoped, Lenin led agitation for an immediate end to the war and a further, more extreme revolution. His slogan was "Bread, Peace and Land."

After the failure of the Kerensky offensive, the Russian Army began to fall apart. Soldiers deserted in the thousands, or formed revolutionary committees and ignored orders from their officers. In Petrograd, a complex political struggle ended in November when the Bolsheviks overthrew the provisional government and set up their own revolutionary government with Lenin at its head. Lenin immediately issued a proclamation advocating a "just and democratic peace" and calling on the people in all combatant countries to revolt against their rulers and end the war. On December 15, the Bolsheviks signed an armistice with the Germans and opened peace negotiations.

The collapse of Russia was a great boost for the Germans, and it was a triumph that they desperately needed, for by this time the United States had entered the war against them. The resumption of unlimited U-boat warfare in February 1917 was a direct challenge to the United States, since many of the ships sunk on their way to British ports would inevitably be American. The Zimmermann telegram (see box), was also interpreted by most Americans as a hostile act.

TURNING POINT

The Zimmermann telegram

On January 17, 1917, the German foreign minister, Arthur Zimmermann, sent the German ambassador in Mexico a proposal for an alliance between Germany and Mexico. The Mexicans were to be encouraged "to reconquer the lost territory in Texas, New Mexico and Arizona" from the United States. Zimmermann did not know that both British and American intelligence services were eavesdropping on transatlantic communications. They intercepted the message. In early March, the contents of the telegram were revealed to the American public. It caused a sensation, turning American opinion decisively against Germany.

Bolshevik leader Vladimir Ilyich Lenin addresses a crowd in Petrograd (St. Petersburg) during the Russian Revolution. Standing alongside the podium on the right of the picture is another leading revolutionary, Leon Trotsky.

U.S. president Woodrow Wilson saw himself as a man of peace. He had been reelected in 1916 with the slogan: "He kept us out of the war." But on April 2, he asked Congress to authorize a declaration of war on Germany, saying: "The world must be made safe for democracy." America entered the war on April 6, although it tried to keep its distance from Britain and France. Instead of joining the Allies, the United States became only an "Associate Power."

Representatives of the Russian Bolshevik government, and of Germany and its allies, meet at Brest Litovsk to sign an armistice. The harsh peace terms imposed on Russia at Brest Litovsk in March 1918 deprived the country of more than a third of its prewar population.

The U-boat campaign at first threatened to achieve all that the Germans had hoped. In April 1917, one in four ships sailing to Britain was sunk. The imports on which Britain depended to survive were being cut off. American troops could never be shipped across to Europe if losses were occurring on such a scale. But in May, Britain introduced a convoy system. Merchant ships crossed the Atlantic in large groups under naval protection. The result was a drop in losses from around 25 percent to 1 percent. The British government was still forced to ration many imported foodstuffs in short supply, but Britain could go on fighting.

The United States had only a small peacetime army. Training and equipping an army to fight in Europe was a slow process, so the Americans had no immediate impact on the fighting. But the entry of the United States into the war and the fall of the tsar in Russia

HOW DID IT HAPPEN?

Why did America join in the European war?

U.S. president Woodrow Wilson presented America's entry into the war as an act of idealism. He claimed that the United States had no selfish motive—not even "to defend our territory"—but was acting as "the champion of right and liberty."

Some historians have challenged this idealistic view of American action, arguing that the United States exploited the opportunity presented by the war to increase its economic and political power. Specifically, providing Britain and France with supplies had become vital to the American economy. Americans had also lent the Allies very large sums of money to pay for these supplies. The United States had to ensure that the Allies did not lose the war, or the loans would never be repaid and the U.S. economy would suffer.

Other historians have argued that German domination of Europe would have been a long-term threat to American security and therefore had to be resisted. However, no one has produced any documentary evidence to show that Wilson had other than idealistic motives.

American soldiers about to set off on the long journey to Europe say farewell to their families. More than 2 million Americans eventually crossed the Atlantic, giving a massive boost to the Allied war effort.

together had a profound effect on war aims. The Allies were now able to present their war as a struggle for democracy, freedom, and national self-determination—the right of national groups to govern themselves. This had not been possible while the tsarist regime—an enemy of democracy and ruler of many nations within its empire—was an ally.

The changing situation also encouraged antiwar feeling in Germany. For many Germans, the main motive for supporting the war had been fear of conquest by tsarist Russia. With the threat of the tsar gone, in July 1917, the German Reichstag (parliament) voted in favor of a peace resolution. But the Reichstag did not have control over the German high command. Encouraged by the collapse of Russia, in November 1917, Ludendorff and his colleagues decided that, in the following spring, they would launch a final colossal offensive on the Western Front. They believed that they could win the war in 1918.

6 The Final Battles

On March 3, 1918, the Russian Bolshevik government signed a peace treaty with the Germans at Brest Litovsk. It was a humiliating agreement that the Bolsheviks only agreed to sign because the Russian Army had dissolved and they were defenseless against German military might. Russia was forced to accept the loss of two-fifths of the population of the former Russian Empire. Poland; Ukraine; Belarus; Finland; Moldova; the Baltic states of Lithuania, Latvia, and Estonia; Armenia; Azerbaijan; and Georgia all became independent, at least in principle. In practice, they were subject to strict control and ruthless economic exploitation by Germany and Austria-Hungary.

Dead British soldiers lie in a trench captured by the Germans in the offensive of spring 1918. Initially a triumph for Germany, the offensive eventually exhausted the German Army and exposed it to counterattack.

VOICES FROM THE PAST

Fight to a finish

In April 1918, British military leaders seriously feared that their army might be facing defeat. The British commander, Field Marshal Douglas Haig, issued a ringing proclamation to his troops, who were bearing the weight of the German offensive:

"With our backs to the wall and believing in the justice of our cause, each one of us must fight to the end. . . . Every position must be held to the last man."

Quoted in John Keegan, *The First World War* (Hutchinson, 1998)

The harsh terms imposed on Russia convinced even many Germans that Germany's rulers were fighting a war of conquest, not of self-defense. There was a wave of strikes in German and Austro-Hungarian factories by workers who sympathized with the Bolsheviks and demanded a just peace.

For the German high command, however, the triumph in the east presented the opportunity to transfer troops to reinforce the Western Front. The Germans knew that they had to exploit the advantage this gave them quickly—before American soldiers began to arrive in Europe in large numbers. On March 21, 1918, masses of German troops supported by over 10,000 artillery guns and mortars launched an offensive against the British armies on the Somme. Known as the Michael offensive or the *Kaiserschlacht* (Kaiser's battle), it was initially an overwhelming success. The British lines were ripped apart. The long stalemate on the Western Front was at an end. Follow-up offensives in April and May carried the Germans to within less than sixty-five miles of Paris.

As early as March 23, a triumphant Kaiser Wilhelm granted all German schoolchildren a holiday to celebrate "Victory Day." Yet after initial panic, the Allies rallied in the face of the overwhelming onslaught. For the first time in the war, British and French forces were joined under a single commander in chief, French general Ferdinand Foch. Despite their gains of territory, the Germans suffered heavy losses—348,000 in the first six weeks of the offensive. The Allies also lost hundreds of thousands of

American soldiers fight on the Western Front. Their arrival meant that, despite the heavy casualties suffered by Britain and France in the battles of spring and summer 1918, the number of troops on the Allied side continued to grow.

men, but enough American "doughboys"—the nickname for the American infantry—were arriving in Europe to replace them. About 200,000 U.S. troops landed in France in the month of May alone. Commanded by General John Pershing, they fought their first action against the Germans at Chateau-Thierry on the Marne in early June.

French tanks advance toward the war zone in 1918. The large-scale use of tanks by the Allies in 1918 helped break the stalemate.

Through the early summer, the Germans continued to attack, but with diminishing success. By August, the Allies were ready to launch a counteroffensive. On August 8, Canadian and Australian infantry, supported by 350 tanks and over 2,000 aircraft, attacked at Amiens, pushing the Germans back and inflicting heavy casualties. Ludendorff called it "the black day of the German army." Two days later he told the kaiser that Germany could no longer hope to win the war.

Through the following months, the Allies launched a series of successful offensives that, by early October, had carried them beyond the Hindenburg Line into territory the Germans had held since 1914. The Allies were far superior to the Germans in the use of tanks, which had now developed into a major force on the battlefield, and their planes dominated the air, bombing and strafing German soldiers and supply lines. The freshness of the American troops also contributed to the Allied success, although their inexperience meant they often suffered especially heavy casualties. The Germans, meanwhile, worn down by years of fighting and demoralized by the failure of their spring offensive to win the war, began to surrender in increasing numbers.

The Central Powers Collapse

Away from the Western Front, Germany's allies were crumbling. In the Ottoman Empire, the British had captured Jerusalem in December 1917 and, in September 1918, decisively defeated Turkish forces at the Battle of Megiddo. On the Italian front, the Austro-Hungarian Army was in disarray after a last failed offensive in the summer of 1918. In the Balkans, an Allied army, advancing north from the Greek port of Salonika, attacked Bulgaria on September 15. The Bulgarians surrendered within two weeks.

On September 29, Ludendorff told the kaiser that Germany must seek an immediate end to the fighting. There were as yet no foreign troops on

General John Pershing (left) was the commander of American forces in Europe. He did not agree with President Woodrow Wilson's desire for a compromise peace, instead arguing for a total military victory and for the imposition of harsh terms on Germany.

TURNING POINT

Wilson's fourteen points

On January 8, 1918, President Wilson announced a fourteen-point plan for a just peace. Some of the points were proposals for a better postwar world. For example, general disarmament would cut all countries' arms to the minimum required for national defense, and an international organization would be set up to guarantee countries against attack by their neighbors. Other points were more specific. Germany was to hand back territory occupied during the war, as well as Alsace-Lorraine. Poland—previously divided up between Germany, Austria-Hungary, and Russia—was to become an independent state. National groups in the Austro-Hungarian and Ottoman empires were to be given autonomy—not full independence, but a large say in running their own affairs. The existence of Wilson's peace plan became a major factor in ending the war in the autumn of 1918.

British troops formally occupy Jerusalem, Palestine, in December 1917. Palestine had been ruled by the Turks as part of the Ottoman Empire, but after the war it came under British administration.

German soil, and the German line on the Western Front was unbroken. The German leaders hoped that they could still make a deal that would enable them to claim to be undefeated. On October 4, they told Wilson that they accepted his fourteen-point peace plan and asked him to arrange a cease-fire.

By negotiating with Wilson, the German leaders hoped to get lenient terms. But the British and French, as well as American military leaders, made certain that an armistice was offered only on tough conditions, designed to ensure that the Germans could not start fighting again at a later date. German territory west of the Rhine was to be occupied by Allied forces, and large quantities of Germany military equipment were to be handed over to the Allies. Some German military leaders, including Ludendorff, wanted to reject these terms and fight on. But the kaiser dismissed Ludendorff on October 26.

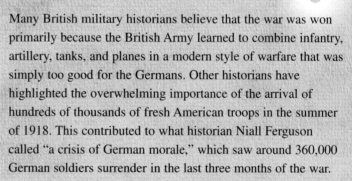

HOW DID IT HAPPEN?

Why did Germany lose?

Many British military historians believe that the war was won primarily because the British Army learned to combine infantry, artillery, tanks, and planes in a modern style of warfare that was simply too good for the Germans. Other historians have highlighted the overwhelming importance of the arrival of hundreds of thousands of fresh American troops in the summer of 1918. This contributed to what historian Niall Ferguson called "a crisis of German morale," which saw around 360,000 German soldiers surrender in the last three months of the war.

By contrast, after the war, many Germans held the view that their army had never been defeated on the battlefield at all. Ludendorff in particular claimed that the German Army had been "stabbed in the back" by politically motivated groups at home who undermined the war effort. But historian A.J.P. Taylor countered that losing the war caused a revolution, not the other way around: "The German revolution . . . was caused by Ludendorff's confession that the war was lost."

Niall Ferguin, *The Pity of War* (Penguin, 1998); A.J.P. Taylor, *The First World War* (Penguin, 1963)

In practice, the worsening political situation inside Germany made continuing the war an impossible option. The German people were suffering dire hardship. Largely as a result of the British naval blockade, there were chronic shortages of food and fuel. The country was seething with unrest. When, outraged by the armistice terms, naval commander Admiral Reinhard Scheer ordered the German fleet to set sail for a final showdown with the Royal Navy, the sailors refused to obey. Instead, the port of Kiel was taken over by revolutionary sailors and workers. In early November, major cities across Germany fell under revolutionary control.

Austria-Hungary was in even worse condition, because popular unrest similar to that in Germany was accompanied by ethnic divisions. With the encouragement of the Allies, the country's Poles, Czechs, and other Slav minorities began organizing their own governments and claiming areas of Austro-Hungarian territory. By the time Austria-Hungary signed an armistice with the Allies on November 3, the Austro-Hungarian Empire had already effectively ceased to exist.

On November 9, Germany was proclaimed a republic and the kaiser abdicated, fleeing to exile in the Netherlands. Two days later—still protesting about the terms they were being forced to accept—a German delegation signed the armistice in a railway carriage in the Compiègne Forest in eastern France. The guns fell silent on the Western Front at eleven o'clock on November 11, 1918.

This photograph shows recently captured German prisoners of war at Abbeville, France, in August 1918. The fact that German soldiers began to surrender in large numbers indicates how demoralized they had become.

7 A Failed Peace

The announcement of the armistice on November 11, 1918, was greeted by the countries on the winning side with unbridled celebrations. Delirious crowds filled the streets in major cities such as London, Paris, New York, Chicago, and Melbourne. But even among the victors were millions of people in no mood to celebrate —especially those in mourning for realtives lost in the war. In much of the rest of the world, defeated and devastated, there was no cause for rejoicing at all.

No one knows for certain how many people died in the First World War. The total number of men killed in the fighting is estimated at between 8.5 million and 9.8 million. Germany lost over 2 million men on the battlefields, Russia probably 1.8 million, France 1.4 million, Austria-Hungary over a million, Britain and its empire around 900,000, Italy almost half a million, and the United States 50,000. Those who died in battle were mostly young men. Of German men who were between the ages of nineteen and twenty-two when the war started, one in three died.

The war also took a heavy toll in civilian casualties. According to some estimates, for example, 700,000 German civilians may have died through hardship and malnutrition during the war and in its aftermath, mostly as a result of the British naval blockade which was maintained until June 1919. Some small countries suffered disproportionately. Around 600,000 Serbian civilians and perhaps half a million civilians in Romania are thought to have perished as a result of the effects of the war.

Even more people died as a result of a virulent influenza epidemic, which was a by-product of the war. This flu probably first appeared on the Western Front in the spring of 1918. Spreading worldwide during 1918–1919, it killed 20 million people, including 62,000 U.S. soldiers.

French people flood onto the Parisian boulevards to celebrate the armistice on November 11, 1918. There were similar scenes in London and other major cities in the countries on the winning side.

The Peace Treaties

In January 1919, the leaders of the victorious powers gathered in Paris for a peace conference. The defeated nations were not invited. Proceedings were dominated by the "Big Four": Britain, France, the United States, and Italy. U.S. president Wilson aimed to create a new

VOICES FROM THE PAST

"The dead were dead . . ."

Vera Brittain served as a nurse during the war, in which some of her closest friends and family were killed. On the evening that peace was declared, she went out with some colleagues to mingle with celebrating crowds in central London. She later wrote:

> "Wherever we went a burst of enthusiastic cheering greeted our Red Cross uniform, and complete strangers . . . rushed up and shook me warmly by the hand. . . . I detached myself from the others and walked slowly up Whitehall, with my heart sinking in a sudden cold dismay. . . . The war was over; a new age was beginning; but the dead were dead and would never return."

Vera Brittain, *Testament of Youth* (Virago, 1978)

At Brookwood Cemetery in Surrey, southern England, people visit the graves of dead soldiers on a memorial day in June 1919. The graves of American soldiers buried in the cemetery have been marked with American flags.

order in Europe based on democracy and self-determination—the redrawing of borders so that each ethnic group could live under its own national government. The French prime minister, Georges Clemenceau, by contrast, wanted above all to weaken Germany so that it could not attack France again in the future.

Diplomats look on as the peace treaty with Germany is signed in the Hall of Mirrors at Versailles on June 28 , 1919.

A French gunboat keeps watch over the Ruhr River during the occupation of part of Germany in 1923.

Of the series of peace treaties made with the defeated countries, the most important was the Versailles treaty with Germany. Under its terms, the Germans had to hand back Alsace-Lorraine to France, as well as give up a modest amount of other territory—for example, giving Poland access to the sea by a corridor across German territory to the port of Danzig (Gdansk). The German Army was limited to 100,000 men, with no tanks or aircraft. The Germans were to pay reparations to Britain, France, Italy, and Belgium to compensate for the damage these countries had suffered. And they had to admit that the war had been a result of German aggression—this was known as the "war guilt clause." German representatives signed the peace treaty on June 28, 1919, but only after the Allies had threatened to resume the war and invade Germany.

The peacemakers in Paris had little or no control over most of the changes that resulted from the war. Amid the ruins of the Russian, Austro-Hungarian, and Ottoman empires, competing groups fought to establish new borders and regimes. New states, including Finland, Poland, Czechoslovakia, and Yugoslavia, were created by nationalist groups. The borders of the new states were mostly decided by local wars. For example, Poland extended its territory eastward in 1920 by winning a war with Russia.

Inside Russia, civil war raged between the Bolshevik government and its enemies from 1918 to 1920. This immensely destructive conflict ended with the Bolsheviks in control of the majority of the territory of the former Russian Empire, which became the Soviet Union in 1922. There was also warfare in Turkey, where nationalist leader Kemal Ataturk deposed the Ottoman sultan to found a Turkish republic and defeated an attempt by Greece to take a large slice of Turkish territory. Britain and France between them reorganized the rest of the former Ottoman Empire (the British, among other things, creating the new Arab state of Iraq).

The borders that resulted from the peace conference and from these postwar conflicts did not fulfill Wilson's ideal of national self-determination. For example, Austria was forbidden to unite with Germany, although its population was overwhelmingly German. Wilson's idea for an international organization to

The first meeting of the League of Nations takes place in Geneva in 1920. The failure of the United States to join the new international organization partly undermined its effectiveness from the outset.

VOICES FROM THE PAST

Ripping up the treaty

In April 1939, German dictator Adolf Hitler described how his political career had been dedicated to undoing the Versailles treaty:

"I have . . . endeavoured to destroy sheet by sheet the treaty which . . . contains the vilest oppression which peoples and human beings have ever been expected to put up with."

J. Fest, *Hitler* (Weidenfeld & Nicholson, 1973)

maintain peace in the future was, however, adopted. The League of Nations was intended to ensure that all countries would unite against any state that resorted to war. But when Wilson went back to the United States after the peace conference, the U.S. Congress refused to ratify the peace treaty, arguing that belonging to the League of Nations might involve America in future European wars. The

By 1923, the countries of Europe had settled into a new shape. Germany lost some territory, mostly to Poland and France. Part of Germany—East Prussia—was cut off from the rest of the country by a strip of territory, giving Poland access to the sea at Danzig (Gdańsk). The breakup of the Austro-Hungarian Empire left Austria as a small country of mostly German population.

failure of the United States to join the League of Nations weakened the organization from the outset.

The First World War left a legacy of discontent and bitterness. The attempt to force Germany to pay reparations, which led to the occupation of the Ruhr district of Germany by France and Belgium in 1923, plagued international relations in Europe. The world economy, disrupted by the war and its aftermath, could not recover its prewar stability and plunged into the Great Depression in the late 1920s. Germany was especially hard-hit by the Depression and the mass unemployment that came with it.

Right-wing German nationalists—such as Nazi Party leader Adolf Hitler—blamed most of his country's misfortunes on the Versailles treaty. After Hitler came to power in Germany in 1933, neither Britain and France, nor the League of Nations, was prepared to prevent him from rearming Germany and embarking on a policy of armed expansion that led to the Second World War in 1939. Hitler's aim was essentially to reverse the results of the First World War. His defeat of France in 1940 was sealed by a humiliating peace agreement, signed in the same railway carriage used for the signing of the armistice in November 1918.

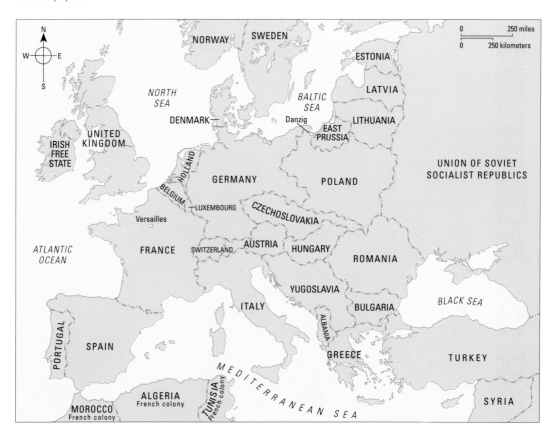

The First World War had utterly failed to be "the war to end wars," as some had hoped at the time. But it did change attitudes about warfare. When the Second World War started, there were no cheering crowds to be seen in European cities—not even in Nazi Germany. The sacrifice of the millions who died on the Western Front was not forgotten. It is still remembered in annual ceremonies today, even as the last few survivors of those who fought in the war fade away.

HOW DID IT HAPPEN?

Guilt of the peacemakers?

The German delegates who reluctantly signed the Versailles treaty in 1919 protested at "the unheard of injustice of the conditions of peace." Whether the peacemakers at Versailles really treated Germany too harshly has been the subject of intense debate. Influential British economist J.M. Keynes thought so at the time. In his 1919 book *The Economic Consequences of the Peace*, he wrote: "The Peace [Treaty] is outrageous and impossible and can bring nothing but misfortune."

According to historian Niall Ferguson, however, the peace terms were not especially harsh and "Germany came out of the war no worse off than Britain, and in some respects better off." A large number of historians have felt that the treaty, although far from perfect, was probably the best that could have been achieved under the circumstances of the time. A.J.P. Taylor, for example, pointed out that the way the Germans were treated was inevitable, writing: "A peace of reconciliation" would have meant accepting "that there was nothing to choose between the two sides and that the only fault of the Germans was to have lost. Who dared say that at the time? Who, outside Germany, would say it now?"

German quote from Martin Gilbert, *A History of the Twentieth Century* (HarperCollins, 1997); J.M. Keynes quoted in Niall Ferguson, *The Pity of War* (Penguin, 1998); A.J.P. Taylor, *The First World War* (Penguin, 1963)

Adolf Hitler, the leader of the Nazi Party, had fought in the trenches in the First World War. After coming to power in Germany in 1933, he rebuilt the country's military strength and set out to reverse the result of the war—an ambition that led to an even more devastating global conflict—World War II.

World War I Time Line

1914

June 28: Assassination of Austrian archduke Franz Ferdinand

July: Austria-Hungary declares war on Serbia

August 1: Germany declares war on Russia

August 3: Germany declares war on France

August 4: Britain declares war on Germany

November 16: The Ottoman Empire enters the war on the side of the Central powers

November 22: The First Battle of Ypres ends in stalemate

1915

April 25: Allied forces land at Gallipoli, Turkey

May 7: The *Lusitania* is sunk by a German U-boat

May23: Italy enters the war on the Allied side

December 19: Allied troops begin evacuation from Gallipoli

1916

February 21: The Germans launch a massive offensive against the French at Verdun

May 31: Battle of Jutland

July 1: Beginning of the Battle of the Somme

August to December: Romania enters the war and is swiftly defeated by the Central powers

1917

February: Germany begins an unrestricted U-boat campaign

March: Collapse of the tsarist regime in Russia

April 6: The United States declares war on Germany

July: A final Russian offensive in Galicia fails; the Russian Army begins to disintegrate

July 31 to November 6: The Third Battle of Ypres, or Battle of Passchendaele

November 7: The Bolsheviks seize power in Russia

December 15: Russia and Germany agree to an armistice

1918

January 8: U.S. president Wilson announces his fourteen-point peace plan

March 3: The Treaty of Brest Litovsk

March 21: The Germans launch a massive spring offensive on the Western Front, driving the Allies back toward Paris

October 28: Mutiny by German sailors at Kiel triggers revolutionary uprisings across Germany

October 30: The Ottoman Empire signs an armistice with the Allies

November 3: Austria-Hungary signs an armistice

November 9: Germany is declared a republic and the kaiser flees into exile

November 11: Germany signs an armistice; fighting stops on the Western Front

1919

June 28: The signing of the Versailles treaty

Glossary

abdicate To step down from a throne, giving up the right to rule a country.

Allies Term used for Britain, France, and the other countries fighting on their side during the war.

annex To take over territory.

armistice An agreement between two sides in a war to stop fighting so they can negotiate a peace treaty.

atrocities Massacres or other acts of extreme brutality.

autonomy A degree of self-government falling short of full independence.

Central powers Term used for Germany, Austria-Hungary, and their allies.

colonial empire System in

which European countries such as Britain and France ruled extensive territories in other parts of the world.

Commonwealth An international association consisting of the United Kingdom together with states that were—at the time of the First World War—part of the British Empire—and dependencies.

conscription Compulsory service in the armed forces.

dominion A self-governing country in the British Empire.

ethnic divisions Conflicts or disagreements between people of different national, racial, or religious groups living in the same country.

munitions Ammunition and other equipment needed by an army.

no-man's-land The area between the front line of two armies, for example between the opposing trenches on the Western Front.

Ottoman Empire A Turkish-ruled empire that controlled much of the Middle East.

outflank To advance around the side of an enemy position.

reparations Payments demanded from a defeated country by the victors to compensate for damage they have suffered in war.

self-determination The principle that people should be ruled by their choice of government.

shell shock Psychological disturbance caused by prolonged exposure to bombardment.

strafing To fire on troops on the ground from an aircraft.

U-boat A German submarine.

For Further Information

Books

Simon Adams, *World War I*. New York: Dorling Kindersley, 2004.

Peter Bosco, *World War I*. New York: Facts On File, 2003.

Sean Connolly, *World War I*. Chicago: Heinemann, 2003.

Stephen Currie, *Life in the Trenches*. San Diego: Lucent, 2002.

Adrian Gilbert, *Going to War in World War I*. New York: Franklin Watts, 2001.

R.G. Grant, *World War I: Armistice 1918*. Chicago: Raintree, 2001.

Stewart Ross, *Causes of World War I*. Chicago: Raintree, 2003.

Gail B. Stewart, *World War I*. San Diego: Blackbirch, 2004.

Web Sites

Encyclopedia of the First World War (www.spartacus.schoolnet.co.uk/FWW.htm).

FirstWorldWar.com (www.firstworldwar.com).

The Great War and the Shaping of the 20th Century (www.pbs.org/greatwar).

World War I: Trenches on the Web (www.worldwar1.com).

Index   Page numbers in **bold** indicate photographs